Witchcraft in England

Ursley Kemp?

Witchcraft in England

CHRISTINA HOLE

Drawings by Mervyn Peake

B. T. Batsford Ltd
London

First published 1977

© Christina Hole 1977

ISBN 0 7134 0277 6

Photoset in 11 on 12pt. Janson
by Weatherby Woolnough,
Wellingborough, Northants
Printed in England by
J. W. Arrowsmith Ltd, Bristol
for the publishers
B. T. Batsford Ltd
4 Fitzhardinge Street, London W1H 0AH

Contents

Searched for Devil's marks

1 Witchcraft in England

Witchcraft was known in England, as in most other countries of Europe, from time immemorial. We hear of it before the country that now bears that name was England at all, both in pre-Roman times, and during the centuries between 43 BC and AD 410, when Britain was part of the great Roman Empire. The Romans, indeed, had their own stern laws against the practice of magic, especially charms and incantations intended to harm ordinary people, or any attempts made to discover the length of the Emperor's life. (Centuries later, it was still a serious offence in England to try to divine how long the King would live.) When Christianity first began to spread slowly through the land in early Anglo-Saxon times, the official view of witchcraft was radically changed by the attitude of the Church. Hitherto, magic directed to evil ends had been regarded as dangerous and evil in itself, but white magic, that is magic used for good purposes only, had not. Now the Church taught that it was all essentially evil, black and white alike, because it involved an appeal to powers beyond those of God, a presumptuous attempt to compel by human arts benefits which could be granted or denied only by the Divine Will. Moreover, it was closely associated with paganism, and usually it involved consulting with demons, who were the most dangerous enemies of all Christians.

As early as towards the end of the seventh century, Theodore, then Archbishop of Canterbury, drew up his *Liber Poenitentialis*, one of the earliest known collections of English ecclesiastical laws, which included a number of punishments ordained for forms of witchcraft apparently prevalent at that time. None of them was severe. Sacrifices made to demons merited penance from one to ten years. If a man killed another by spells, he had to do penance for seven years, during three of which he must fast on bread and water. Astrologers who invoked demons for the purpose of sending a man mad had to fast on bread and water for a year, and also serve four more years of penance; and oddly enough, the same punishment was prescribed for the, surely, far less serious crime of raising storms.

In the following three or four centuries, the anti-witchcraft laws slowly stiffened. King Edgar, in the mid-tenth century, ordered every priest in the land to promote Christianity with the utmost zeal, 'and totally extinguish every heathenism'; and among the 'heathenisms' to be destroyed, he listed 'necromancies, and divinations, and enchantments, and man-worshippings, and the vain practices which are carried on with various spells . . .'. A little later, the Witan of King Ethelred, following the laws of Edward and Guthrum, directed that wherever witches, magicians, and certain other offenders, were found in the land, they should be 'diligently driven out of this country, and this people be purified; or let them totally perish in the country, unless they desist, and the more deeply make bot.'[1]

William the Conqueror declared his own views on witchcraft before he had actually earned the title of Conqueror, and while his final victory over King Harold was still uncertain. On the morning of the Battle of Hastings, he accidentally put his *lorica* on back to front. This was a very bad omen, and some of his followers shook their heads about it, but William roundly declared: 'If I believed in sorcery, I should not go to battle today; but I have never put my trust in sorceries, nor loved sorcerers. For in every business, whatever I had to do, I have always committed myself to my Maker.'[2] Nevertheless, four years later, when Hereward and his friends were successfully defying him in the Isle of Ely, he was persuaded, rather against his will, to try the effects of witchcraft as a possible means of dislodging the rebels.

In *De Gestis Herwardi Saxonis,* it is related that Ivo Taillebois, one of his knights, said he knew of a powerful witch, who might be profitably employed to cast spells over the Saxon enemy, and at the same time encourage his own men. William, in spite of his usually strong views on this subject, seems to have agreed to the suggestion, and the woman was secretly sent for. She was lodged at Brandon, in the house of a widow who, apparently, let lodgings to any likely comer to the parish. While she was staying there, a potter came to the house, and lodged there also. He was, apparently, an illiterate Saxon, travelling simply to sell his goods where he could, and the two women, assuming that he knew no language other than his own, did not scruple to talk French quite freely before him. This, from their point of view, was a mistake, since the man was no ordinary potter, but Hereward himself, disguised, and out to discover whatever he could about the plans and activities of his enemies. He heard them both plotting together, and speaking of the King's intentions; and when, about midnight, they went down to a spring in the garden to seek 'responses' from its indwelling spirit, he followed them, unseen, and heard all that passed.

In due course, when William was ready to make his next assault the witch was set on the top of a high wooden tower, where all could see and hear her. She began to cast spells in a loud voice upon the English, which must have struck terror into the hearts of all but the boldest, in that age when practically everybody believed in the powers of witches. But Hereward was prepared; and as she began her third high chant, the English under his command set fire to the reeds which grew everywhere in that place.

A strong wind was blowing at the time, and in a very short while, the startled Normans saw dense clouds of smoke and swiftly-moving flames sweeping down upon them. They fled, 'each man for himself', as the author of *Gestis Herwardi* tells us, but they could not find their way through the swamps and morasses of that watery countryside. Many were drowned in their flight, and many others perished in the showers of English arrows. The rout was complete, and even William came near to death in the general confusion. As for the witch, she died also, and her magic could not save her, for in the same account of the event we read how 'that woman aforesaid of infamous art in the great alarm fell down head first from her exalted position and broke her neck'.

During the troubled period from the thirteenth century onwards, when the Church was fighting the spread of heresy everywhere, and witchcraft was, slowly but steadily, acquiring a darker look, England was fortunate in that she was without the Inquisition. That powerful organisation could not work freely without the support of the secular authorities of the country in which it functioned, and England had had the great good sense to refrain from inviting it to establish itself here. At the beginning of the fourteenth century, when Philip the Fair, King of France, attacked the Knights Templar for reasons of his own, and accused them of sodomy, blasphemy, and idolatry, certain Inquisitors were admitted into this country, as a special concession, for the purpose of examining the members of the Order here. They did not, however, succeed in obtaining any confessions from the accused men, because the use of torture was not permitted by the Common Law of England. It was, indeed, used upon occasion, but only when sanctioned by an act of the Royal Prerogative, which was not forthcoming in this case. It can scarcely be doubted that the activities of the Inquisition did a very great deal to fan the fears of the people, especially in the later period, when the Inquisitors had been able to extend their labours to straight witchcraft cases; and their absence from the English scene probably helped very considerably to keep down the level of prosecution here, long after the persecution-mania was already raging elsewhere.

It was not until the reign of Queen Elizabeth I that serious witch-hunting really began in this country. It is true that in 1542 a very severe Statute was enacted, which forbade, amongst other things, the conjuration of spirits in order to discover the whereabouts of buried treasure, the making of magical images intended to bring harm to others, and the pulling down of crosses. All these practices, and others of the same type, were alleged to be increasing everywhere, and perhaps, in that time of change and unrest, they were. Nevertheless, little use seems to have been made of the punitive clauses of this Act, and five years later, Edward VI repealed it in the first year of his reign.

In 1563, another Witchcraft Act was passed, somewhat milder than its predecessor of Henry VIII's reign, but altogether more effective in its results. About this time, the general fear of witchcraft seems to have increased considerably, which some scholars have ascribed to the return of the Marian exiles to this country on the accession of Elizabeth. When Mary Tudor came to the throne, many of the more extreme Protestants had been obliged to leave England, and to seek refuge in Calvinistic towns on the Continent, such as Geneva, or Zurich, and others, where a fierce witch-persecution was raging. It is suggested that when it was safe for them to come home, they brought with them continental notions of the nature of witchcraft, and of the manner in which it should be treated. This theory may well be correct, though other scholars have questioned it. In any case, there is no doubt that it was from the passing of the 1563 Act that the real persecution of English witches began.

One of these religious exiles was the Calvinistically-minded John Jewel, who spent several years during Queen Mary's reign in Frankfurt-on-Maine, Strasburg, and Zurich, all centres of a raging witch-persecution at that period. Soon after his return to England, he became Bishop of Salisbury, and one of Queen Elizabeth's advisers. In a letter to Peter Martyr in Zurich, dated 2 November, 1559, he remarked that the number of witches in the land had increased enormously everywhere. In a celebrated sermon preached before the Queen at some time between November 1559 and March 1560, he suddenly broke off from his main thesis in order to warn her against the perils of witchcraft, as he saw them, at that period. He declared that

. . . this kind of people (I mean witches and sorcerers) within the last few years are marvellously increased within your grace's realm. These eyes have seen the most evident and manifest marks of their wickedness. Your grace's subjects pine away even unto death, their colour fadeth, their flesh rotteth, their speech is benumbed, their senses are bereft. Wherefore, your poor subjects' most humble petition unto your highness is, that the law touching such malefactors may be put in due execution. For the shoal of them is great, their doings horrible, their malice intolerable, the examples most miserable. And I pray God they never practice further than upon the subject.[3]

In fact, of course, malicious magic was occasionally extended 'further than the subject', as was only to be expected, and attempts against the life or welfare of the Sovereign are recorded from time to time. Elizabeth herself suffered from them; images supposed to represent her were several times discovered during the course of her reign, though it would seem that they did her no harm. In her father's time, one Mabel Brigge, of York, was executed in 1538 for treason because she had used the deadly ritual known as the Black Fast against King Henry VIII and the Duke of Norfolk. Neither man was affected by her magic, but a rumour spread rapidly that the King was dead. A Mrs Robinson, of Kidderminster, and her two daughters, did their best to prevent the return of Charles II in 1660 by means of spells. All three were arrested and imprisoned in Worcester on 14 May, a little more than three weeks before the King landed in triumph at Dover. They continued to declare until the end that their magical conspiracy would have succeeded if only they had had a little more time.

The Elizabethan Act of 1563 was replaced in 1604 by another Witchcraft Act which was definitely more severe than its predecessor, and introduced new penalties for some forms of necromancy and the consulting, feeding, and rewarding of 'any evil and wicked Spirit'. This increased severity was, and mostly still is, blamed upon James I, in the first year of whose reign the Act was passed. There was a belief, still far from dead, that it was the learned King from over the Border who was, if not the actual instigator, at least the active leader of the whole anti-witch campaign in the early seventeenth century. In this he has been largely maligned. He believed in witchcraft, like the majority of his subjects, Scots and English. He even wrote a book about it in 1597. Nevertheless, he was far less credulous than many of his own judges when it came to particular cases, and it is hardly possible to believe, with justice, that his accession to the throne of England was the signal for a fresh outburst of witch-persecution in that country.

James came from a region where witches had always been more harshly treated than they were in England, and where the notion of devil-worship was more generally accepted. He had, also, his own reasons for believing in the dangerous malice of sorcerers. In 1590, a conspiracy was unmasked, of which the main object was the destruction by magic of the King himself. The instigator of this plot was said to be Francis, Earl of Bothwell, who was the King's cousin, and had some claim to the throne of Scotland should James die without an heir. In any case, the two men were bitter enemies. Bothwell is said to have confessed to his part in the conspiracy, but if he did, his confession has disappeared from the records. He escaped the consequences of his actions by flying to Italy, whence he never returned to Scotland in spite of a pardon granted to him some time later by King James.

His associates in the conspiracy were the witches of North Berwick, the members of a coven which sometimes met in the church of that parish. The plot in which they were all involved was discovered almost by accident. A girl named Gelie Duncan, who was a servant in the house of David Seaton, Deputy-Bailiff of Trenent, suddenly took to absenting herself from her master's house at night and to performing magical cures during the day. Seaton questioned her about this odd behaviour, but getting no answer, resorted to the use of torture (which was possible in Scotland). She still remained obstinately silent, but when she was searched, and an alleged Devil's mark was found upon her throat, she broke down and confessed to the diabolical origin of her healing powers. She was thrown into prison, and there she made further confessions implicating a number of other people, including Dr Fian (or Cunningham), a schoolmaster at Saltpans, and Agnes Sampson, a midwife of Haddington. She alleged that Dr Fian was the leader of the company, and later on, he confessed that he had acted as 'clerk to all those that were in subjection to the Devil's service', recording their names, and taking their oaths, and also leading the witches in their dance round North Berwick church. Still later, he retracted this confession, and everything else he had acknowledged, and in spite of renewed tortures, he could not be made to admit the truth of anything he had previously said. He was still silent when he was executed in January 1591 on the Castle Hill in Edinburgh.

From the confessions and evidence of the accused witches, the details of the plot against the King came rapidly to light. Agnes Sampson acknowledged that she had made a waxen image in his likeness, and had taken it to a small, secret meeting at Prestonpans, where only nine witches were present. The Devil,

The death of the christened cat

their master, being present, she offered the image to him, and when he had approved it, it was passed from hand to hand through all the company, each one saying in turn as he passed it to his neighbour: 'This is King James the Sixth, ordained to be consumed at the instance of a noble man, Francis, Earl Bothwell.' Another method of magical murder planned by the witches was to collect the venom of a toad that had been hanged by its feet for three days, and smear it upon something that the King had worn. This failed because John Kers, one of James' servants from whom Agnes Sampson had begged the necessary garment, or piece of linen, lost his nerve at the last moment, and refused to give it. Then, after the King's marriage, when he was returning from Denmark with his bride, they christened a cat and, after having bound upon it 'the chiefest part of a dead man and several joints of his body', flung the unfortunate creature into the sea to drown. This horrible ceremony was intended to raise a fierce storm that would wreck the ship in which James was sailing. A storm did arise immediately, and a boat coming into Leith (opposite which town the cat had been cast away) was sunk; but evidently the spell was not sufficiently powerful, for the royal ship, though much harassed on the voyage by bad weather, came safely home to Scotland.

James was present at the examination of the prisoners, and listened very attentively to their confessions. At the end of it all, he lost patience, and remarked that 'they were all extreme liars'. Then a very curious thing happened. Agnes Sampson suddenly declared that she would not wish the King to suppose her words were false, and thereupon, drawing him a little aside, she repeated to him the actual words that had passed between him and his bride on their wedding-night in Norway. James was astounded, as well he might be, for there was no normal means by which she, or any other outsider, could possibly have known this. He acknowledged that her words were 'most true', and swore 'by the living God that he believed all the devils in hell could not have discovered the same'.[4]

Whatever the source of her mysterious knowledge may have been, it is clear that the King was deeply impressed by Agnes Sampson's account of what had happened that night. He was, after all, the only person present who knew whether she was telling the truth or not. What drove her into making so dangerous a statement, no one knows. James's freely expressed incredulity must have seemed to offer her (and her fellow-prisoners also) at least a hope of pardon and release; but this she deliberately rejected by going out of her way to admit knowledge that could only be explained by magic. She was, so far as is known, quite sane, nor does she appear to have been one of those hysterical individuals who seek importance at all costs, and at any risk. She must have realised what the effect of such a declaration would be upon her own immediate fate, but nevertheless, she made it, without any sort of provocation or persuasion, and in due course she was executed in Edinburgh. How far it also influenced the King's own beliefs in the powers of witches, we cannot now be certain, but it seems very probably that it strengthened them to a considerable extent.

In 1597, he published his *Daemonologie*, a book in the form of a Dialogue, in which he clearly stated his own views upon certain aspects of witchcraft. This seems to have been written in the first place as a sort of reply, or counterblast, to the sceptical writings of Reginald Scot and Friedrich von Spee. As the work of a reigning king, his book naturally had a fair amount of influence, and in 1604, soon after he had acceded to the English throne, it was re-published in London, where it must certainly have helped to establish his reputation as a witch-hunter amongst his contemporaries. But James had other gifts besides a bent for clear writing. He had an acute and scholarly mind, and if he believed wholeheartedly in the general possibility of witchcraft, he was always extremely cautious in dealing with any particular cases of it that came to his notice. He insisted upon real and adequate evidence in every instance, and his notions of what constituted such evidence were often far stricter than those of his judges.

At the Leicestershire Summer Assizes in 1616, presided over by Sir Humphrey Winch and Sir Randolph Crew, nine witches were condemned for bewitching a boy of thirteen named John Smith, and causing him to have fits. They were all hanged on July 18th in that year. Six more witches, accused of the same crime were still in prison, awaiting trial, when King James arrived in Leicester on a Royal Progress. Hearing of the case, he sent for the boy who was still having fits, and closely examined him. Young Smith faltered in his answers, and the King came to the conclusion that he had never been bewitched at all, a view subsequently supported by the Archbishop of Canterbury, to whom he was sent for further examination. Finally, the boy confessed that he had been lying throughout, chiefly from a love of importance. In the meantime, a dreadful miscarriage of justice had taken place. Of the six witches still awaiting trial, one had died in prison, and the other five were released immediately; but the nine previously condemned had already been executed, and nothing could be done for them. The King sharply rebuked the judges involved in this disastrous affair, a fact that caused not only these particular men, but other judges also, to take more care, during the rest of his reign, in the assessment of evidence in witchcraft trials.

Four years later, a somewhat similar case came to light when William Perry – another thirteen-year-old boy, known as the 'Boy of Bilson' – accused Jane Clarke of enchanting him, and causing him to suffer from violent fits and seizures. This time, the prisoner was acquitted at the Staffordshire Assizes in 1620, and young Perry was examined, not by the King, but by Thomas Morton, Bishop of Lichfield and Coventry. At first, the boy stuck to his story, but having been detected by the Bishop in various forms of trickery he eventually confessed that all his fits were simulated, and that he had begun them at the bidding of a Roman Catholic priest, in order that the latter should appear to exorcise him, and so gain glory for the Catholic Church. Later, he had continued his antics because he enjoyed the attention that they brought him. After this confession, he was made to acknowledge his deception at the next Summer Assizes at Stafford in 1621, and to beg forgiveness in public from the woman he had wrongfully accused.

This case, along with several other instances of fraud and pretended possession that came to his notice did a great deal to modify James' views on witchcraft. Dr Fuller, after relating some of these incidents, remarks that 'the frequency of such forged Possessions wrought such an alteration upon the judgement of King James that he, receding from what he had written in his *Daemonologie,* grew first diffident of, and then flatly to deny the workings of Witches and Devils, as but Falsehoods and Delusions'.[5] Here, probably, Dr Fuller exaggerated somewhat, for there is no real proof that James ever completely abandoned his original belief in witchcraft, nor does it seem very likely. Theoretically, no doubt, he continued to hold that there was such a thing, and that people did practise it, in his own day, as in the past; but increasingly, as time went on, his own strong desire for truth and reason prevailed over easy acceptance of the alleged facts whenever some particular case was brought to his attention. His judges may sometimes have dreaded his interventions, but they were always on the side of common sense, and for that reason, though he was not a particularly merciful man, they frequently resulted in the saving of innocent lives.

The Act of 1604 remained in force until 1736, when it was repealed, and a new law, forbidding the prosecution of any person for witchcraft, conjuring, and similar offences, was enacted. This was the final flowering of a tendency that had been growing steadily since the time of the Restoration. Though the ordinary people seem to have remained as fiercely hostile as ever to every alleged witch (as their behaviour at some of the later trials clearly indicated), it is evident that amongst the better-educated the witch-mania was slowly dying out. After 1660, many more trials ended in acquittals or reprieves than formerly, and fewer executions are recorded. Charles II, like his father and grandfather before him, usually took a tolerant view of witchcraft matters, and in any case, was far more interested in the scientific findings of the Royal Society, of which he was Patron, than in magic. The influence of such men as Chief Justice Holt, that courageous and sensible judge who secured the acquittal of every witch he tried, began to spread very widely, and so did that of certain books, such as John Webster's *Displaying of Supposed Witchcraft . . .* (1677), and still more, Francis Hutchinson's *Historical Essay concerning Witchcraft* (1718).

The last English execution for the crime of witchcraft was that of Alice Molland, who was hanged at Exeter in 1684.[6] The last witch to be condemned to death (though she did not die) was Jane Wenham, of Walkern, in Hertfordshire. She was tried in 1712 by Sir John Powell, who obviously doubted her guilt, though, naturally, he could not say so. He did his best to restrain his jury, but in this he failed, and they brought in a verdict of guilty. This being so, he was forced to condemn her to death, but he managed to delay the execution, and during the time thus gained, he obtained a royal pardon for her. While all this was happening, a lively battle of pamphlets and printed letters was being waged between those who believed her to be a genuine witch, deserving of death, and those who questioned the whole matter and being of witchcraft, and were therefore

convinced of her innocence. Her life was saved by the Queen's
pardon, and by Sir John Powell's diligence in obtaining it; but
she was never again able to live in her own village, where all the
inhabitants remained quite certain that she was a dangerous
witch, whatever the Judge and other outsiders might have to say
on the matter.

In 1717, a woman named Jane Clarke was committed, along
with her son and her daughter, for trial at Leicester, after being
subjected to certain traditional witch-tests, like scoring above the
breath and swimming; but no trial followed in this case because
the Grand Jury threw out the Bill. Nineteen years later, the Act
of 1736 removed the crime of witchcraft from the Statute Book,
and made the prosecution of any person supposedly guilty of it
impossible. Thus, the English witch-persecution was brought to
an end, after it had lasted for 173 years, from the reign of
Queen Elizabeth I to that of George II; and if there were many
at that time who felt that the new Act was dangerous, ill-
conceived, and contrary to the teachings of the Bible, there is
little doubt that the majority of thoughtful people were only too
glad to see the old, harsh laws against so uncertain a crime as
witchcraft swept away for ever.

Persecution in England was never, even at its worst, quite as
savage, or as widespread, as its Continental counterpart, but it
was, nevertheless, horrifying enough. It is not certainly known
how many accused witches perished during that dreadful period,
either in European countries or in England, but certainly the
English figures were very much lower, both relatively and
actually. Those who died were hanged, not burned, as on the
Continent and in Scotland. It is true that instances of witches
burnt to death do exist in this country, but never for witchcraft
alone. In every case, that crime was associated with heresy,
poisoning, or treason, and so was liable to the more drastic
penalty. Thus, Mary Lakeland was burnt alive at Ipswich in
1645 because she had murdered her husband (amongst others),
and the murder of a husband by a wife (or a master by a
servant) was petty treason, punishable by burning. 'Several
other things she did', says the writer of a contemporary tract,
'for all which she was by Law condemned to die, and in particular to be burned to death, beçause she was the death of her
husband, as she confessed . . .'.[7]

Torture to enforce confession, widely used in most other countries, was illegal in England, though some of the tolerated forms of ill-treatment seem to have been almost as dreadful. An accused person, man or woman, who had been watched for several days and nights, starved, bullied, kept without food or sleep, ceaselessly walked up and down, searched for the Devil's Mark, or subjected to the 'swimming test', was likely to confess whatever his accusers demanded of him in order to bring the torment to an end. Quite often, such confessions were retracted as soon as the wretched prisoner had had time to recover a little, but the retraction rarely did him any good. The confession had been made, and the method of obtaining it was not usually allowed to weigh against its probably truth, except by a few more enlightened magistrates. It is true that, even in the height of the witch-mania, most trial-judges insisted upon some sort of supporting evidence for the confession itself, and some outside proof of the prisoner's guilt; but it can never have been very easy for them.

For one thing, almost any sort of evidence was then deemed acceptable, including hearsay. A single witness's testimony was sufficient for a conviction, and that witness might be a known enemy of the accused, or an obviousy hysterical or unreliable person, or a child. By Law, he had to be at least fourteen years old, but this rule was often ignored. Jennet Device was only nine when she gave evidence against her mother and her brother at Lancaster in 1612. About twenty years later, in the same county, Edmund Robinson, a lad of ten, bore witness against a number of alleged witches, though in this case the Assize Judge showed himself rather less willing to accept his testimony than his predecessor in the earlier trial had been with Jennet Device. Neither the Boy of Bilson, nor John Smith, of Leicester were as yet of the statutory age to give evidence against any one, though both were allowed to do so without any one even commenting upon the illegality of this course.

Witnesses for the defence were, of course, readily heard, but very often those who might have come forward were afraid to do so. The prisoners were not always able to speak up clearly for themselves, through ignorance, or confusion, or perhaps through sheer terror; and in any case, witchcraft was a crime of which it was exceedingly difficult to prove innocence. Even a strong alibi was of little use, since most people believed it possible for a witch to appear to be in one place when he or she was in fact somewhere else. Moreover, the noise and clamour which was quite common in the court-room during a trial often made it impossible for the prisoners to make themselves heard. Aubrey records that when Anne Bodenham was tried at Salisbury in 1653, 'the crowd of spectators made such a noise that the judge could not hear the prisoner, nor the prisoner the judge; but the words were handed from one to another by Mr R. Chandler, and sometimes not truly reported'.[8] Similarly, Mary Spencer (one of Edmund Robinson's victims) complained to Bishop Bridgeman that 'she would have answered for herself, but the wind was so loud, and the throng so great that she could not hear the evidence against her'.[9] Added to all this was the fact that some judges were themselves ardent believers in witchcraft, and so were inclined to accept as 'proofs of guilt' evidence which a non-believer might have rejected. By difficulties of this kind, the course of strict justice must constantly have been hampered, even in the hands of the most upright and experienced judges.

After 1736, witch-trials ceased, and with them the circulation of those lurid and exciting pamphlets allegedly containing the Full Confession of some wretched individual newly condemned to death (and frequently decorated with alarming illustrations of demons and familiars) which did so much to fan the fears of simple people. It need hardly be said that faith in the existence of witches did not die out immediately, since age-old beliefs cannot be swep away at once by a simple Act of Parliament. People continued to suppose themselves overlooked or enchanted by malicious witches when things went wrong for many years thereafter; and sometimes to take strong action on their own account against the suspected culprit, since they could no longer obtain redress from the Law. Assaults, duckings, scoring above the breath, occasionally even murder, went on as before, though less frequently, with the difference that now it was the perpetrator of the violent act, and not the supposed witch, who was prosecuted. White witches also continued to flourish, and are by no means extinct as yet, though in many cases now their activities are limited to the use of particular charms, or the healing of certain diseases, rather than the general magical powers of former years.

21

Gradually, however, the old notions died away, and witchcraft ceased to be a serious menace, as it had once been. Today, where it exists at all, it is a mere shadow of its former self. It is true that, of late years, a modern cult has come into existence, which claims to be directly derived from the witch-religions of long ago. Its members assert that they are worshippers of Diana, or of the Horned God, and that their wide knowledge of ancient magic is never used for anything but good. However that may be, there does not seem to be any very close connection between this cult and the historical witchcraft of the English past, except, possibly, that the witches believe in their own powers as firmly as their predecessors did. One great difference, of course, is that unlike those predecessors, they are free to practise their art without any fears of legal reprisals.

Witch hanging

The Horned God

2 Witchcraft and Religion

The Christian Church in the early centuries sternly condemned every sort of witchcraft, the white no less than the black, and forbade all magical practices as relics of paganism; but at the same time, it displayed a strong tendency to disbelieve in the actual powers of magicians, and its general attitude towards practitioners of magic was far less harsh than it afterwards became. Bishops worked hard to suppress every instance of sorcery they encountered, but they also taught that no true Christian needed to fear the effects of witchcraft, since magic was outside God's pattern for the world, and therefore could not succeed. If it seemed to do so, that was due to delusions caused by demons, whereby the magician also was deceived, no less than his victims. It was a sin to believe otherwise, for that meant that the believer was opening his mind willingly to diabolic fantasies, but if any one resolutely refused to do this, then he or she was quite safe from any real danger from the malice of witches.

About the year AD 906, the famous *Canon Episcopi* appeared in a collection of ecclesiastical documents made by Regino, Abbot of Prum. It was long thought to be a canon of the Council of Ancyra, held in AD 314, but in fact, this was not the case, and its actual origin is still uncertain. It was, however, of great importance during the Middle Ages, and, in the twelfth century, it was incorporated in the *Corpus Juris Canonici* of Gratian de Bologna, and thus became part of accepted Canon Law. It dealt primarily with the supposed nocturnal rides of women with Diana, and also with the matter of shape-shifting, and firmly condemned belief in either. The relevant passages concerning the night-ride ran:

> ... It is also not to be omitted that some wicked women, perverted by the Devil, seduced by illusions and phantasms of demons, believe and profess themselves, in the hours of night, to ride upon certain beasts with Diana, the goddess of the pagans, and an innumerable multitude of women, and in the silence of the dead of night to traverse great spaces of earth, and to obey her commands as of their mistress, and to be summoned to her service on certain nights. But I wish it were they alone who perished in their faithlessness and did not draw many with them into the destruction of infidelity. For an innumerable multitude, deceived by this false opinion, believe this to be true, and so believing, wander from the right faith and are involved in the error of the pagans when they think there is anything of divinity or power except the one God. Wherefore the priests throughout their churches should preach with all insistence to the people that they may know this to be in every way false and that such phantasms are imposed on the minds of infidels and not by the divine but by the malignant spirit.[1]

In this passage there is no reference to witchcraft as such. The women mentioned were deluded, 'seduced by illusions and phantasms of demons' into believing themselves to be the night-travelling servants of a pagan goddess. Their sin lay, not in anything they did (for what they were supposed to do was impossible), but in their ready acceptance of these devilish delusions, and the consequent encouragement of false belief in others. They did not actually ride with anybody, divine or demonic, but perhaps influenced by their own lurid dreams, and an ancient legend of a night-hunt still current in their time, they thought that they did. But they were not witches, and the compiler of the *Canon Episcopi* did not say that they were. Nevertheless, in the course of time, they did become confused in the popular mind with witches; Diana became a devil instead of a pagan goddess, and the nocturnal journey over immense distances a forerunner of the aerial flight to the Witches' Sabbat.

Perhaps because of this 'quality of disbelief', the Church's early penalties for witchcraft were comparatively lenient. Witchcraft was always considered a serious crime, but it was a crime amongst others, ranking with perjury, adultery, and incest. A person accused of it was allowed to prove his innocence, if he could, by Ordeal. In the *Liber Poenitentialis* of Theodore, the seventh-century Archbishop of Canterbury, periods of penance and fasting varying from one to ten years were laid down for offences ranging from sacrificing to demons, or the destruction of a man by means of evil spells, down to raising storms by magic, or the use of divination. The secular laws enacted by various Anglo-Saxon kings were usually more severe, including the punishment of exile in very serious cases, and death for some forms of secret magical murder; but for a long time very few trials for witchcraft were heard in the civil courts. Like paganism, or heresy, sorcery and divination were considered religious matters, and judgement therefore lay principally in the hands of the Church.

The early ecclesiastical leniency could not last for ever, and, in fact, it did not. The situation slowly altered, and at the same time the attitude of the Church hardened, and became much more severe. Tales of witchcraft became more lurid as time went on, both those that were told in sermons and the writings of the learned, and those that circulated by word of mouth in cottage and ale-house. The power of Satan seemed to be growing. As the old heathen beliefs slowly faded and were forgotten, so the ancient gods of paganism were increasingly replaced in men's minds by the Devil and his attendant fiends. The famous story of the Witch of Berkeley apparently dates from this period, and William of Malmesbury goes so far as to state that he had heard it from some one who saw the whole thing happen in 1065.

There was a woman living at Berkeley, in Gloucestershire, who was a witch, and had a familiar spirit in the form of a bird. She also had a married son, and two other children, one of whom was a monk and the other a nun. One day, her familiar (a jackdaw according to William of Malmesbury, but according to some other versions of the tale, a chough) told her that her married son and all his family had been killed in an accident. She took this to be a sign of God's vengeance upon her for her many and terrible sins, and sending for her two surviving children, she told them there was no hope at all of saving her soul from Hell, but if they would follow her instructions carefully, they might be able to save her body. When she died, they were to sew up her corpse in a stag's skin, and lay her on her back in a stone coffin. On the top of the coffin, they were to put a heavy stone, bound round with strong chains. They were then to cause psalms to be said for her for fifty nights without stopping, and masses to be said on fifty consecutive mornings. If, as a result of all this, her body remained quietly in the grave for three days and nights and was not disturbed, they could be sure that all was well, and the corpse could be safely buried in the graveyard.

When the witch died, her children did as she asked them, but it was all of no avail. Notwithstanding the psalms and the masses, and the stag-skin sewn round the body, on the same night as she was laid in the stone coffin, a demon of great height broke into the church, followed by a company of other fiends. They pushed aside the great stone on the coffin-top, breaking the chains that bound it with the utmost ease, opened the coffin, and commanded the dead woman to rise. She did so, and dragging her out of the building, they forced her to mount upon a black horse that was waiting outside, and forthwith rode away with her. She was never seen again.[2]

In his *De Nugis Curialium*, Walter Map records a curious tale of what appears to have been a sort of vampirism in the twelfth century. An English knight named Sir Walter Laudun came to the Bishop of Hereford, Gilbert Foliot, to seek advice. He said that in the Welsh Border town where he lived, a sorcerer (a Welshman) had recently died, but he did not rest in his grave. He came back every night and called by name one or two of his former neighbours; those whom he called at once fell ill, and died within three days. Night after night, these terrible visitations were repeated, and men and women continued to die in this strange manner. The Bishop, after giving the matter due thought, advised Laudun to have the dead witch's body dug up, beheaded, and then re-buried in the same grave, after this had been thoroughly well dowsed with holy water. This was done, but it had no effect at all. At last, one night, Sir Walter's own name was called, whereupon the knight, seizing his sword, boldly pursued the living corpse back to the churchyard and, with a single terrific sword-stroke, managed to cut off its head before it could reach the shelter of its grave. It never afterwards returned to harass the people of the town.

In 1301, Sir John Lovetot suddenly brought some very terrible accusations against Walter Langton, Bishop of Coventry, who was also Treasurer of England. He charged him with simony and other ecclesiastical offences, with adultery committed with his (Lovetot's) stepmother, and the murder of his father, old Sir John Lovetot, by causing him to be secretly strangled in his sleep. In addition to all this, he alleged that the Bishop was a sorcerer, and that he had made a pact with Satan, to whom he had rendered the obscene homage of the posterior kiss. This was an accusation which was to be heard in many later witch-cases, the kiss *a tergo* being often thought to be a regular ceremonial of the witch-cult. Langton fiercely denied all these charges, but the case dragged on for two years, to the great fury of Edward I, who supported his Treasurer strongly throughout. The Bishop was summoned to Rome by Pope Boniface VIII, and was kept waiting about there for several months without anything being settled. Finally, he was tried in England by a special commission over which the Archbishop of Canterbury presided. In 1303, he was acquitted. All the charges made against him were declared to be false, including sorcery, diabolic pact, and the murder of Sir John Lovetot; but he required the help of thirty-seven compurgators to clear himself, and was forced to borrow a very large sum of money to cover his expenses while he was detained in Rome. It is extremely probable that politics, and also personal malice, played a large part in this unusual affair, but the case is interesting in itself for the light it sheds upon current notions concerning the connection between sorcery and Satanism during the reign of Edward I.

From the twelfth century onwards, the spread of heresy in Europe, and the efforts made by the Church to suppress it, had an increasingly important effect upon the general attitude, both clerical and lay, towards witchcraft. When, round about 1230, the Inquisition was founded for the extirpation of heresy, it was not at first allowed to deal with witchcraft as such; but, by the fourteenth century, it had established its right to do so by evolving the theory that witchcraft was itself the blackest of heresies, since it necessarily involved a personal pact with Satan, and homage paid to him. From this, it was only a short step to belief in a new devil-worshipping sect of witches, recently come into being, whose members were obliged to renounce God and adore His arch-enemy, and who were themselves active black magicians and dedicated enemies of all good Christians.

Many of the wild and horrific accusations brought against Catharists and other heretics were repeated in charges made against witches. They were said to be guilty of ritual murder, of stealing and kidnapping children, of wholesale immorality and carnal intercourse with demons, and blasphemies of every kind. All the old stories of nocturnal flight (now supposed to be to great meetings, or Sabbats, of the new cult) and metamorphosis appeared again in a new form, and the *Canon Episcopi,* which forbade belief in either, was neatly by-passed by the witch-hunters, who argued that the original *Canon* had referred only to wrongful opinions held in the past, and not to the witch-sect, which did not exist at the time when it was written. They asserted also that it was possible even for dreams to be heretical, if they were demon-inspired, and the dreamer willingly consented to them. And while such tales circulated freely, so belief in the actual powers of witches steadily increased.

In 1484, Pope Innocent VIII issued the famous Bull, *Summis desiderantes affectibus,* in which he vigorously denounced the evil works of witches, and made it quite clear that the Inquisition's activities against such criminals had full papal support. This was not the only papal Bull of its kind. Earlier in the fifteenth century, Eugenius IV and Nicholas V had issued others of the same sort, but the importance of *Summis desiderantes affectibus* lay, at least partly, in its active support of Heinrich Kramer (or

Institoris) and Jakob Sprenger. These were two Inquisitors who in 1486 produced the celebrated book, *Malleus Maleficarum* – the 'Hammer of Witches'. This sinister volume was intended by its authors to refute every possible argument against the reality of witchcraft. It described in detail almost all the crimes commonly alleged to be committed by witches, together with methods of discovering them, and the manner in which they should be punished. By our standards, it was a cruel and vicious book, but those who read and used it when it first appeared did not think so. It became a handbook for the guidance of judges and magistrates, and ran into fourteen editions between 1486 and 1520.

The natural result of all this was a great increase in the popular fear of witchcraft, and a steady rise in the number of trials. By the end of the fifteenth century, the anti-witch craze was already raging in many European countries, and it did not die away completely until the end of the seventeenth or the beginning of the eighteenth century. Once witchcraft had been defined as heresy, the way was open everywhere for a full-blooded persecution. While it lasted, few people were altogether safe from suspicion; even children were not exempt, for they were often supposed to be trained up to follow their witch-parents, or to be offered to the Devil in infancy, or at about seven years old.

Nicolas Remy, one of the Provosts of Nancy between 1576 and 1591, and an experienced judge, stated in his book, *Demonolatry,* that the children of condemned witches were frequently 'stripped and beaten with rods round the place where their parents were being burnt alive'. He had himself sentenced children to this inhuman punishment, and he did not consider it went far enough. He believed that quite young children could, and did, commit criminal acts of sorcery, and that therefore, 'out of consideration for the public safety, such children ought in addition to be banished and exiled from the boundaries of human nature . . . for experience has shown that they who have fallen into the power of the Demon can rarely be rescued except by death . . .'.[3]

About seventy-five years after Remy's book first appeared, an outbreak of witchcraft, in which many children were apparently involved, came to light in Sweden. Reports of very strange doings at Mohra, in Elfdale, caused the King of Sweden to appoint a Royal Commission to enquire into the matter on the spot. Some seventy adults were accused, of which twenty-three confessed to various witchcraft crimes, and were condemned to die. They acknowledged that they had been accustomed to summon the Devil (whom they called Antecessoar) to meet them at a certain crossroads. When he came, he made them swear to serve him with soul and body, and then he carried them off, 'Over Churches and High Walls', to a place called Blockula, which was a fine house set in a broad green meadow. Many children were of their company, their own and those of other people, about fifteen or sixteen every night, all riding upon goats, or posts, or enchanted men, provided by the Devil. At Blockula, they shared in everything that went on there except that, when the feasting began and the adults sat down to eat at a very long table, the children had to stand in the doorway and wait until Satan himself brought them meat and drink.

About 300 young people, some of them very young indeed, were supposed to be involved in this affair, having been corrupted and brought into the power of Satan by the older witches. The children were all examined separately, to see if their confessions agreed with those of their companions or of the other witches. The Commissioners found that, within reason, they did. Amongst other things, they said that when they were summoned to Blockula, they sometimes went very willingly, and sometimes they refused; but they had to go whatever they said. In the end, fifteen of them were considered guilty enough to die with the twenty-three adults who had confessed. Thirty-six others, 'between nine and sixteen years of age, who had been less guilty', were forced to run the gauntlet, and also to be beaten with rods upon their hands once a week, at the church door, for a whole year. Twenty more, who were younger and 'who had no great inclination, yet had been seduced to these Hellish Enterprises' were also to be beaten on their hands, like the others, but only for three Sundays together, 'because they were young'. But if, as we are told, 'the number of the seduced children was about three hundred', then the great majority of them must have been lucky enough to escape punishment altogether.[4]

In England, where the Inquisition never gained a foothold,

and where the use of torture was illegal, except in very special cases, the concept of a malignant and dangerous witch-cult, dedicated to the worship of the Devil, and the performance of every sort of evil, was very slow to take root. Nothing was heard here of this secret organisation before the sixteenth century, nor did it figure very prominently in English trials during the years that followed its first appearance. Educated men who had read Continental writings on the subject were, of course, familiar with the theory of the supposed new sect, but ordinary people, even when they knew anything about it, which was not always the case, paid but little attention to it. They believed that witches were harmful and wicked, that they consorted with demons, and that normally they made a truly hateful compact with Satan, whereby they gave him their souls and acknowledged him as their Lord in exchange for whatever they most desired in life – money, power, success in love, revenge upon their enemies, or simply great skill in the art of magic. But for the most part, it was felt that witches did these things on their own initiative, with or without accomplices, because they were natural criminals rather than because they were members of a diabolical sect.

Similarly, belief in the Witches' Sabbat, which was widespread in Europe, was never very strong in England. It was assumed in most places where the cult was accepted as a fact that the members of that cult must necessarily meet together from time to time, at small local gatherings to carry on the business of the local organisation, and at greater assemblies held at fairly long intervals, to which all the witches of a given district came. This greater meeting was the Sabbat. It took place at night, usually in the open air, sometimes in a house, as at Mohra, or in the parish church, which had the advantage of being a large building that would certainly be empty and available during the hours of darkness. The Devil presided over it, or at least some one who represented him did so, perhaps a high official of the cult who, disguised and heavily masked, and wearing great horns upon his head, might quite easily be, and probably was, believed by many of those present to be the Evil One in person.

The Sabbat was primarily a religious ceremony. Satan was adored thereat, sacrifice was offered to him, new converts came to swear allegiance and renounce Christianity, and to be admitted as members of the cult, children were dedicated to his service by their parents. Witches reported upon the evil they had done since the last meeting, and new plans were made for the magical destruction of men and animals. At the end of the night, there was feasting, dancing, and singing, and, finally, an outburst of promiscuous sexual intercourse in which male and female witches, demons, and sometimes the Arch-Fiend himself all took part.

Witches came to the Sabbat in various ways. If the meeting-place was near enough to their homes, they probably walked there, or perhaps went on horseback. Margaret Johnson, one of the Pendle women accused by Edmund Robinson in 1634, admitted that although she was not present at 'the great meeting' at Hoarstones on All Saints Day, she had attended another gathering on the following Sunday, at which there were 'between thirty and forty witches, who did all ride to the said meeting'.[5] Twenty-two years earlier, in the same district of Lancashire, James Device had declared that after the Good Friday meeting in 1612, held at Malkin Tower, all the witches there present 'went out of the said House in their own shapes and likenesses. And they all, by that they were forth of the doors, were gotten upon Horseback, like unto Foales, some of one colour, some of another ...'.[6] It is not altogether clear whether the creatures 'like unto Foales' were real horses, or demons in the form of horses sent by the Devil to carry his worshippers to and from the meeting; but perhaps in view of Margaret Johnson's later evidence, given in the same district, we may assume that the 'foals' here were real, and not diabolic.

There were other ways of travelling to the Sabbats, especially to those held too far off for ordinary walking or riding. Witches sometimes rode there upon enchanted men and women, who served them as horses for the time being. In 1673, Anne Armstrong, who lived near Stocksfield-on-Tyne, alleged that she had been so bewitched, and forced to carry certain local witches to the meeting at Riding Mill. In the records of her evidence, we read that 'one night, a little before Christmas, this informant see the said Anne Forster[7] come with a bridle and bridled her, and rid upon her cross-legged till they came to the rest of her companions at Riding mill bridge-end, where they usually met. And when she light off her back, pulled the bridle off this informer's head, now in the likeness of a horse; but when the bridle was taken off, she stood up in her own shape . . .'.[8] Sometimes the witches flew through the air on the backs of beasts who were really fiends in disguise, or else seated upon staves or rods; and often they depended for their powers of aerial flight upon the use of a magical ointment with which they smeared either their own bodies, or the staves upon which they rode.

In 1664, Elisabeth Style, one of the Somerset witches, confessed that before she and her companions went to the Sabbat, 'they anoint their Fore-heads and Hand-Wrists with an Oil the Spirit brings them, which smells raw, and then they are carried in a very short time, using these words as they pass, *Thout, tout, a tout, tout, throughout and about.* And when they go off from their Meetings, they say *Rentum Tormentum*'. Anne Bishop, another witch of the same company, said that 'her Forehead being first anointed with a Feather dipt in Oyl, she hath suddenly been carried to the place of their meeting', and that at the end of the assembly, their leader, the Man in Black, departed and 'the rest were on a sudden conveighed to their homes'.[9]

This was one of the few English cases in which evidence for the use of flying ointments was clearly given. The Somerset witches did not say how the oil was concocted, though one of them described it as of a greenish colour. The general belief seems to have been that such magical salves were composed of a mixture of poisonous herbs of various kinds, and the fat and marrow of dead children who had either been stolen from their homes and murdered or, having died naturally, were dug up from their graves. Francis Bacon, who tended to believe that confessions by witches of aerial flights were due rather to dreams or delusions than to fact, wrote in 1608 that 'the ointment that witches use is reported to be made of the fat of children digged out of their graves; of the juices of smallage, wolfbane, and cinquefoil, mingled with the meal of fine wheat; but I suppose that the soporiferous medicines are likest to do it'.[10] Reginald Scot, who certainly had no faith in Sabbats and flying ointments, thought it worth while to transcribe one method of preparing such an unguent. 'The receipt', he says, 'is as followeth.

R. The fat of young children, and seethe it with water in a brazen vessel, reserving the thickest of that which remaineth boiled in the bottom, which they lay up and keep, until occasion serveth to use it. They put hereunto *eleoselinum, aconitum, frondes, populeas,* and soot. Another receipt to the same purpose. R. *Sium, acarum vulgare, pentaphyllon,* the blood of flittermouse, *solanum somniferum, et oleum.* They stamp all these together, and then they rub all parts of their bodies exceedingly till they look red and be very hot, so as the pores may be opened, and their flesh soluble and loose. They join herewithal either fat, or oil instead thereof, that the force of the ointment may the rather pierce inwardly, and so be more effectual. By this means (saith he)[11] in a moonlight night they seem to be carried in the air, to feasting, singing, dancing, kissing, culling, and other acts of venery (saith he), with such youths as they love and desire most: for the force of their imagination is so vehement that almost all that part of the brain, wherein the memory consisteth, is full of such conceits.'[12]

In her remarkable and influential book, *The Witch-Cult of Western Europe* (1921), Dr Margaret Murray advanced the theory that the supposed new and heretical sect of devil-worshipping witches was, in fact, neither new nor heretical, but was a survival of a pre-Christian fertility cult that had once existed in Europe, and possibly in Egypt also, but had been driven underground by the advent of Christianity. Dr Murray was a distinguished Egyptologist and an anthropologist, and she approached the whole subject of witchcraft from the standpoint of anthropology. She saw that Christianity had gained ground only very slowly in the majority of regions, and that even after it appeared to be firmly established in any given place, beliefs and practices clearly rooted in ancient paganism continued to flourish secretly for a very long time. The worship of wells, trees, and stones persisted in spite of every effort the Church could make to suppress them. The forbidden dance of the animal-men still went on at the Kalends of January, and there were many instances of sacrifice offered to the old gods whenever trouble threatened, or Christian prayers had apparently gone unanswered. Old fertility beliefs struck very deeply into men's hearts, and were not easily uprooted; women clung to tried pagan customs at marriage or childbirth; and even the usually devout sometimes tried to get the best of both worlds by reverting in secret to the older rites upon occasion. The Venerable Bede records that, in the seventh century, King Redwald of the East Saxons maintained two altars in the same temple, one for Christian worship, and another, smaller one for sacrifice to pagan gods.[13]

Occasionally, also, witches confessed to adoring a non-Christian god – Dianus (or Diana), or Cerunnos, the Horned God, or other deities whose names varied in different districts. In Guernsey, he was called Hou, in the Basque country, Janicot. In 1596, Marian Grant, of Aberdeen, said that Christsonday was the name of her Lord, by whom she had been commanded to worship him on her knees. Andro Man, a member of the same coven, confessed that 'Christsonday came to him in the likeness of a fair angel and clad in white clothes, and said he was an angel, and that he should put his trust in him and call him Lord and King'.[14] At Stapenhill in Derbyshire, at about the same time, Elisabeth Wright, being called upon to help her daughter, Alse Gooderidge, in healing a sick cow belonging to a man named Michael, agreed to do so 'upon condition that she might have a penny to bestow upon her god, and so she came to the man's house, kneeled down before the Cow, crossed her with a stick in the forehead, and prayed to her god, since which time the Cow continued well'.[15] The name of the god is not recorded. There are other instances of the same straightforward paganism in witches' confessions; but more commonly, accused witches acknowledged as their Leader some mysterious stranger, some Man in Black such as the Somerset covens venerated in 1664, or some unidentified fiend, and perhaps the Devil himself.

Dr Murray believed that all this, and much else of the same sort, simply illustrated the continued existence of an organised cult, handed down through centuries from the remote past. The organisation itself was elaborate, based upon local groups (or covens) usually made up of thirteen persons, and including people of all classes, from the king downwards. It was not a heretical cult, for the simple reason that it had nothing to do with Christianity as such. It was a religious community quite independent of the Church, and far older than that body, and all its dances and orgies, its Sabbats, pacts, and other distinctive features, so horrifying to the Christian observer, were simply the ceremonies and customs of an ancient and altogether different faith.

This theory would account for many things in the history of witchcraft that are otherwise not easy to understand. It would explain the curious uniformity of the confessions, with all their striking details of initiation, sacrifice, and homage to a central horned figure. It would account for the organised covens, the Sabbats at regular intervals, the search for converts and the ease with which these converts were apparently obtained. It would account also for the courage shown by many accused witches, and their refusal to repent, even in the face of a horrible death. And it is perhaps easier to accept the existence of such a cult than the theory, still advanced by some writers, that thousands of simple and ignorant people practised witchcraft because they were conscious Satanists, willingly devoting themselves to the adoration of the Evil Principle. Satanism is a perversion of the intellect fortunately beyond the mental scope of most ordinary men and women; and a theory which rests upon the idea of widespread Devil-worship, in many countries at once and over a long period of time, is as frankly incredible as the wildest stories of witches flying to the Sabbat upon broomsticks, or changing themselves into hares or cats or foxes at will.

Nevertheless, it is difficult to conceive how any organised and active pagan cult could, in fact, have survived practically unchanged, against the opposition of Church and State, from pre-Christian times down to the eve of the eighteenth century. Nor does there really seem to be sufficient evidence that it actually did so. If some witches confessed to alien worship, the majority did not. The charms and spells which Dr Murray herself called Operative Magic (as distinct from Ritual Magic), were practised at all times by every sort of individual, including many whose sincere Christianity could not be doubted. The performance of time-honoured fertility rites did not necessarily mean that the performer was a conscious follower of the older gods, though it did usually mean that he or she was sharing in something frowned upon by the Church for moral or doctrinal reasons. In Scotland, in 1282, John, the priest of Inverkeithing, led the young girls of his parish in a phallic dance of decidedly obscene character during Easter Week. For this, penance was laid upon him, but the punishment was not severe, and he was allowed to retain his benefice.[16] Soon afterwards, he was murdered by an enraged parishioner who presumably felt that the Church authorities had been altogether too lenient in this case. But probably they were right, since it is quite likely that the priest was simply remembering some ancient magical custom, long known in his district, without recalling anything very clearly about the pagan sources from which that custom sprang. We do much the same thing when we dance, or encourage our children to dance round the undoubtedly heathen Maypole in Spring, but no one now accuses us of paganism, or heresy, or witchcraft, nor do we feel ourselves guilty of any of these things.

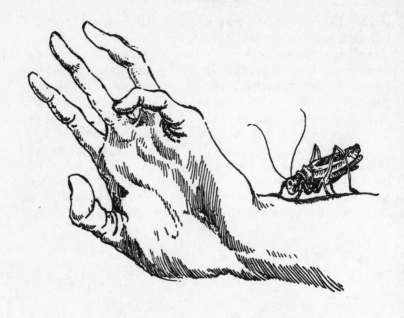

3 Familiars and Shape-Shifting

Few ideas were more firmly rooted in the popular mind during the latter years of the witchcraft-belief than the notion that all witches possessed familiar spirits which they had received from the Devil, and by whose aid they practised divination and magic. Spirits had, of course, been invoked by magicians from a very early period, and made to serve their will. Solomon had command over the hosts of the air; the Witch of En-dor, like other necromancers, was able to recall the dead for her own ends, and those of Saul; sorcerers everywhere, with circle and pentagram and elaborate ritual, called up still more terrifying citizens of the spiritual world, not always with complete immunity from danger to themselves. The gods and nature-spirits of paganism were both worshipped and magically invoked, and when eventually they became confused in men's minds with the demons of the Christian era, later witches could still call upon them for occult purposes. But all these were not familiar spirits in the accepted sense. They came, and they went again; magic constrained them to appear, but their chief business was elsewhere. The fairies also, those indeterminate beings who occupied a shifting border-line between good and evil, were often consulted by magicians, and sometimes taught them a little of their own secret arts, but their assistance was only intermittent, and they always reverted at their will to their own subterranean existence.

The familiar spirit of popular belief was not quite the same as these various inhabitants of remoter worlds, who might be summoned and commanded for a time, by those who knew how to do it, but could not be possessed. The familiar was personal to the witch, one of the lesser demons of Hell, assigned by the Devil at initiation or some other time, or given by some older magician who no longer needed its services. Sometimes it was inherited, passing from one generation to another in a family, usually from mother to daughter. The Widow Bridge, who about 1667 was living in Castle Street, Liverpool, as one of Sir Edward Moore's tenants, inherited a familiar from her mother, and so did her sister, Margaret Ley. An entry in the Moore Rental records that the latter,

. . . being arraigned for a witch, confessed that she was one, and when she was asked how long she had so been, replied since the death of her mother; who died thirty years agone, and at her decease she had nothing to leave her and this widow Bridge, that were sisters, but her two spirits, and named them, the elder spirit to this widow, and the other spirit to her, the said Margaret Ley.[1]

The writer of this entry piously adds: 'God bless me and all mine from such legacies. Amen.'

Gifts of familiars between unrelated witches were not un-known, and there is even an instance of a sale recorded in 1337, in the Manor Rolls of the Isle of Axeholme. Robert de Roderham complained that he had paid three pence to John de Ithen for a 'devil', and had not received it. Apparently, 'the said John . . . did not deny the agreement', but, 'because it appeared to the Court that such a suit ought not to subsist among Christians, the aforesaid parties are therefore adjourned to the infernal regions, there to hear their judgement, and both parties were amerced . . .'.[2]

The familiar spirit could appear in a great variety of forms, from that of a man down to an insect, but most often it came as a cat, or a dog, or any small animal that could easily be given house-room. Richard Bernard, the author of *Guide to Grand Jury-Men* (1627), declared that 'witches have ordinarily a familiar, or spirit, in the shape of a Man, Woman, Boy, Dog, Cat, Foal, Fowl, Hare, Rat, Toad, etc. And to these spirits they give names, and they meet together to Christen them.' Occasionally, a ferret is mentioned in a witch's confession, or in evidence, or a weasel, a polecat, a rabbit, or a mole, and sometimes, though rarely, a bird, like the spirit called Tewhit who was attached to Margaret Thorpe, of Fewstone, in 1621, and was 'yellow of colour, about the bigness of a crow'.[3]

It was these small domestic familiars which were employed by the witches for working magic, and which were sent by them on mischievous errands, to harm or destroy the property, and sometimes the persons, of those who had offended them. They were rewarded for their work with drops of the witch's blood, or were fed by sucking at some supernumerary nipple on the witch's body. The discovery of such a nipple during examination was commonly regarded as a proof of guilt, since it was supposed to have been bestowed by the Devil for the express purpose of feeding the spirit-beast. In an age when a fondness for small animals was nothing like as general in England as it is now, the actual possession of any beast that might be supposed to be a familiar was a clear danger to any person suspected of witchcraft, especially if he or she was known to treat it with affection. It was not even necessary for the creature to live in the house; a dog bounding towards a suspected person in the fields, or a cat jumping through a window might be enough to confirm an already existing suspicion. At the trial of the Bideford witches in 1682, one witness said he had seen a cat jumping through a window in the house of one of the prisoners, and evidently thought this simple statement to have some value in the case. Roger North relates in his account of the trial that he, 'sitting in the court the next day, took up the file of information taken by the justices, which were laid upon the table, and against one of the old women read thus: "This informant saith he saw a cat leap in at her (the old woman's) window, when it was twilight; and this informant further saith, that he verily believeth the said cat to be the devil, and more saith not".'[4]

At the trial held at Chelmsford in 1566, two women confessed to having possessed, at different times, the same familiar, in the form of a white spotted cat whose name was Sathan. Elisabeth Francis, of Hatfield Peveril, said she had received it

Elisabeth Francis with toad

from her grandmother, Mother Eve, also of Hatfield Peveril, who was now dead. It was, she said, this Mother Eve who had first taught her the art of witchcraft when she was twelve years old. When she gave her the cat, she told her to call him Sathan, to feed him on bread and milk, and to keep him in a basket. All this Elisabeth did, and the cat served her faithfully for many years. He spoke to her 'in a strange hollow voice', which she understood because she was used to it, and every time he did anything for her, 'he required a drop of blood, which she gave him by pricking herself, sometime in one place and then in another, and where she pricked herself remained a red spot which was still to be seen'.[5]

She first asked Sathan for wealth, and he brought her eighteen black and white sheep, which she kept for a time, but afterwards they 'did all wear away, she knew not how'. Next, she demanded that Andrew Byles, a local man of some wealth, should marry her, and Sathan promised that he would, only she 'must first consent that this Andrew should abuse her, and so she did'. However, when it came to the point, Andrew refused to marry her, whereupon she caused her familiar to waste his goods, and eventually, to kill him, mysteriously, by a touch on his body.

Later, the cat procured another husband for her, one Christopher Francis, to whom she was still married at the time of the trial. He was not as rich as Andrew Byles, but he was, apparently, better than no husband at all. It does not, however, appear to have been a happy marriage. Elisabeth seems to have yearned for a quiet life, a curious desire for a witch, and one that her own temperament must have made practically impossible for her. She complained bitterly, that 'they lived not so quietly as she desired, being stirred . . . to much unquietness and moved to swearing and cursing'. Her baby irritated her, perhaps because it, too, was 'unquiet', and given to crying; Sathan killed it, at her request. Later on, he lamed her husband by changing himself into a toad and hiding in the man's shoe. Francis inadvertently touched it with his foot, 'and was forthwith taken with a lameness whereof he cannot be healed'.[6]

After she had kept the cat for fifteen or sixteen years, Elisabeth gave him to a neighbour called Agnes Waterhouse, who was afterwards tried at Chelmsford at the same time as herself. This woman employed him to destroy other people's cattle, and to kill William Fyne, who had offended her, by afflicting him with a wasting disease whereof he died. She also confessed that, finding her marriage somewhat difficult, she desired Sathan to kill her husband, which he did, 'about nine years past, since which time she hath lived a widow'. It is interesting to notice that, although no one ever seems to have remarked upon anything strange about Sathan's appearance or habits, it is clear that he lived far beyond the usual span of a cat's life. We do not know how long Mother Eve had him, but probably long enough to know his worth. Her daughter kept him for fifteen or sixteen years, and he was still hearty and

Agnes Waterhouse with her spotted cat

vigorous when she handed him over to Agnes Waterhouse. The latter had him for at least nine years, by her own confession, and probably much longer. Yet although all these women lived in Hatfield Peveril, and Sathan lived with them, one after the other, no inhabitant of the township ever seems to have noticed the cat's extraordinary longevity.

Another cat-familiar belonged to Dorothy Ellis, a Cambridge-shire witch, who confessed in 1647 that

> . . . about thirty years since, she being much troubled in her mind, there appeared unto her the Devil in the likeness of a great cat and speak to this examinant and demanded of her her blood, which she gave him, after which the spirit in the likeness of a cat suck upon the body of this examinant.[7]

Thereafter the cat was at her command. With its help, she bewitched and killed some cattle belonging to Thomas Hitch, and lamed John Gotobed who had been imprudent enough to call her an old witch and throw stones at her. The recorded confession does not state what injury she had received from the family of Thomas Salter, but her revenge was severe. Through the cat, she lamed his wife, and then afflicted his little girl, a baby of some fifteen months old, with violent fits. These seizures continued for three months, and then the child died, whereupon her grandmother laid an information against the witch. We hear no more of the cat after Dorothy Ellis was arrested. Many familiar spirits seem to have deserted their owners once the latter became entangled with the Law, and to have been unwilling, or perhaps unable, to help them while they were in prison. The confession of Margaret Johnson, of Pendle Forest, whom Edmund Robinson accused in 1634, ends with a disillusioned statement that might have been made by numerous other witches also, in which she complained 'that since this trouble befell her, her spirit hath left her, and she never saw him since'.[8]

This spirit did not appear in animal-form, but as a man whose name was Mamilion, and whom she addressed as 'Mamil, my god'. He it was who contracted with her to give him her soul, and then he would supply all her wants and bring her whatever she needed. Similarly, it was 'a thing like a Christian man' who persuaded Anne Chattox, one of the earlier Pendle witches, to give up her soul in exchange for freedom from want. In 1682, Susannah Edward, of Bideford in Devon, related how she had first encountered the Devil some two years earlier when out walking in a field called Parsonage Close, she saw what she took to be a gentleman dressed all in black. He drew near and spoke to her, and she curtseyed politely to him, 'as she did use to do to gentlemen'. He asked her if she was a poor woman, and she replied that she was, whereupon he said that if she would only grant him one request, she need never want again for meat or drink or clothing. But when, surprised at this strange promise, she cried out, 'In the name of God, what is it that I shall have?' the 'gentleman' instantly vanished away.[9]

In 1645, Ellen Driver, of Framlingham, in Suffolk, confessed that many years before, when she was still a young girl, the Devil had come to her in the form of a man with cloven feet. He persuaded her to renounce God and the Church, and afterwards he married her. Pride, she said, was the reason she consented to this ill-omened union. She lived with him for three years, and bore him two children, both of which were changelings. Then he died, or at least, so she thought, though at the time of her trial, sixty years later, she seemed somewhat uncertain on this point. The wretched woman had been 'watched' for three days and two nights before she confessed, and was probably half delirious; but it is possible that her confession may have been based on confused memories of a husband, or a lover, of her youth who first taught her the elements of witchcraft.

Occasionally, the stranger whom the witch encountered turned out to be neither a man nor a demon, but one of those whom Robert Kirk described as 'the Intermediate Unconfirm'd People (betwixt Man and Angel)',[10] in other words, a fairy. Belief in the existence of fairies was still common all over Great Britain in the seventeenth century, though exactly who or what the fairies were never seems to have been quite clear. The many stories told of them give a picture both shifting and uncertain. The fairies themselves were sometimes confused with the spirits of the dead, or with ghosts and poltergeists, or with nature-spirits and half-forgotten heathen deities, with fallen angels, or with the survivors of ancient Neolithic tribes who were believed to linger on still in remote and secret places. They were generally supposed to inhabit a subterranean kingdom which lay below and alongside our material world and to some extent corresponded with it, but was distinct from it. It could be reached occasionally through caves and hillsides, but these entrances were very hard to find, and the Fairy Kingdom itself was a dangerous place to visit. Time ran differently there, as it did in the Kingdom of the Dead, and some who visited it, as they supposed, for a single day, or at most, for two or three days, found on their return home that many years had elapsed in the upper world. And sometimes they found that their own strength and vitality had been mysteriously drained from them while they were away in Fairyland, so that now they pined and became silent and morose, and did not live long after their return.

Fairies were not always visible to human beings, and when they were, they were usually indistinguishable from those about them. From the accounts given by those who had dealings with them, it appears that, although their manner of life was in some ways very splendid, in others it closely resembled that of ordinary people in this world. The men hunted and fished, kept cattle and sheep and dogs, worked in wood or stone or metal, forged weapons and occasionally fought amongst themselves. The women brewed and baked, cooked, spun thread, and laundered like any other housewives, and sometimes borrowed the necessary implements from their mortal neighbours when their own had gone astray. They sometimes sought the aid of human midwives, or nurses, and generously rewarded those who helped them in their need; and sometimes, also, they inter-married with human beings, as the many traditions of young girls carried off to Fairyland, or of fairy wives living with their mortal husbands in Middle Earth, abundantly testify. Neverthe-less, however nearly they touched this world and its inhabitants, and however kindly they showed themselves to be upon occasion, fairies were always feared, and contact with them was never free from danger. They were creatures of alien origin and unpredict-able habit, and as such, their enmity and their friendship were both alike dreaded by the majority of simple folk.

Witches were associated with fairies in most people's minds, as having a natural affinity with them. Both were skilled in magic, and used it for good or evil, as they liked. Both were feared by their neighbours, and condemned by the Church, before and after the Reformation. The prehistoric arrow-heads known as elf-bolts were used by fairy and witch alike to harm men and animals; they inflicted an invisible wound, of which the victim languished and died, unless an antidote could be found and used in time. Witches brought to trial were sometimes accused of consorting with the fairies, or confessed to having visited the King and Queen of Faerie, or the Queen of Elfhame. In 1431, Joan of Arc's examiners, in their attempt to prove her a witch, accused her of dancing round the Fairies' Tree near her home when she was a child, and hanging garlands upon it. Fairies were supposed to haunt this tree, but St Joan denied that she had ever seen any, and said that the garlands which she, along with other children of the locality, used to hang there were made in honour of Our Lady of Domremy. She refused firmly to admit that this tree and its fairies were in any way connected with her 'Voices' and her mission, in spite of the strong efforts of her accusers to make her do so.

In 1438, Agnes Hancock was questioned about her association with the fairy-folk. She was a healer, and specialised in curing children's diseases that had been caused by fairy magic. In spite of this, however, she freely consulted the subterranean people whenever she felt in need of advice or information. She claimed that all her cures were effected solely by known medicines and by prayers; but when she was made to repeat these prayers, they were found to contain 'certain strange and unknown words' which she was unable to explain. These words were consequently assumed to be charms taught to her by the fairies.

Joan Tyrrye, a Somerset white witch, admitted under questioning in 1555 that she had one day encountered a fairy in Taunton market, 'and came to him, thinking to make an acquaintance of him, and then her sight was clean taken away for a time, and yet hath lost the sight of one of her eyes'.[11] It seems likely that this was not her first meeting with a fairy, and perhaps with that particular one. She may have visited his dwelling on some earlier occasion, and possibly have touched her eyes accidentally with the magic salve which was used in the care of elfin children. If so, this would account for her being able to recognise fairies in the upper world when they were invisible to every one else. There are many similar stories of human beings being blinded, temporarily or otherwise, for the crime of seeing the fairy folk when they did not wish to be seen.

Eleven years later, in 1566, John Walsh, of Netherberry in Dorset, being charged with witchcraft, confessed that he consulted the fairies from time to time, always in the hills, and usually either at midnight, or between the hours of twelve and one at noon. It was by knowledge gained from them that he was able to tell whether any man was bewitched or not. He also made the rather curious statement that there were three kinds of fairies – the white, the green, and the black – and of these, the black were the worst.[12] Isabel Gowdie, of Auldearne in Morayshire, said in 1662 that she and some others had gone to the Downie Hills, and 'the hill opened, and we came to a fair and large braw room, in the daytime. There are great bulls routing and skoyling there, at the entry, which feared me.'[13] It was there that she saw young lads shaping and trimming arrow-heads with a sharp instrument like a packing-needle, and learnt how to spang these weapons with her thumbnail. Later, she killed a ploughman in this way, and also a woman who was in the same field.

In his *Displaying of Supposed Witchcraft* (1677), John Webster mentions a Yorkshire white witch who was accused in 1653 of effecting cures by means of a powder obtained from the fairies. The man's name is not recorded in the book, but his story is. 'It happened in my time', says Webster, 'and I was both eye and ear witness of the trial of the person accused.' The latter was, apparently, 'a very simple and illiterate person', who was well known locally for the many cures he performed with his white powder, and did not attempt to deny the source from whence that powder came.

When the judge asked him how he first obtained it, he said that one night, coming home from work, and being 'very sad and full of heavy thoughts, not knowing how to get meat and drink for his Wife and Children, he met a fair Woman in fine clothes', who asked him what the trouble was. He told her, and she then said she would show him how to make a good living by curing the sick and ailing, instructing him to meet her on the next night at the same time and place. He did so, and she led him to a little hill on the side of which she knocked three times. The hill opened, and they went in,

and came to a fair hall, wherein was a Queen sitting in great state, and many people about her, and the Gentlewoman that brought him presented him to the Queen, and she said he was welcome, and bid the Gentlewoman give him some of the white powder, and teach him how to use it; which she did, and gave him a little wood box full of the white powder, and bad him give two or three grains of it to any that were sick, and it would heal them, and so she brought him forth of the Hill, and so they parted.

Being further questioned, he said that whenever he needed any more of the fairy powder, he went back to the same Hill, and knocked three times, saying every time, 'I am coming, I am coming', whereupon he was admitted, and more powder was given to him. The judge asked whether it was light or dark inside the 'fair hall', and was told that it was neither, but was 'indifferent, as it is with us in the twilight'. This statement curiously corresponds with that made by one of the Green Children of Suffolk who, according to William Newburgh,[14] strayed into the harvest field at Woolpit in the reign of King Stephen. She said they both came from a country called St Martin's Land, where it was always dusk, and the sun never shone, though they could see a bright country across a very broad river. At the end of this Yorkshire healer's trial, no evil could be proved against him, and the jury, more sane than many similar bodies at that time, acquitted him.

Witches were commonly supposed to be able to transform themselves into wild beasts, or birds, or other non-human creatures, and occasionally they confessed to having done so. This was a persistent notion which lasted among simple folk right down to the nineteenth century. It stemmed originally from the very ancient and once universal belief in the possibility of metamorphosis. Amongst primitive peoples, it was easy to accept this, because for them all living things were closely akin, and they did not make the sharp distinction that we do between the human and animal worlds. Many pagan gods, like Odin or Zeus, were thought to be shape-shifters; so were some great heroes or powerful sorcerers, and some lesser folk also who, through magic or the performance of ritual acts or the putting-on of an animal pelt or a girdle made of human skin, ceased for a time to be human, and became instead a wolf, a bear, a fox, a cat, or a hare. Such changes among ordinary people were usually rare and always sinister and mysterious, and sometimes they were also involuntary, either because of evil magic, or a curse laid upon the person concerned, or because of heredity. Certain families of Ireland and Scotland were said to be descended from seals or wolves or foxes, and it was generally believed until a very late date that those who belonged to such families took the form of the ancestral beast, either periodically and of necessity, or when they felt so inclined. Every nation has its folk-tales in which the ancient concepts of animal-descent and metamorphosis clearly appear – stories of swan-maidens and seal-wives, and legends like those of Melusine and Red Riding Hood – which continued to be told and cherished long after the early stages of culture from which they sprang had ceased. It may be noted that in these old tales and traditions the people concerned were ordinary people (except in so far as their sinister gift was concerned), and by no means necessarily witches; and indeed, it was not until the fourteenth century that shape-shifting became identified with witchcraft.

The reality, or otherwise, of metamorphosis, and its immediate causes when it did occur, were the subjects of much earnest debate among learned men for many centuries. The early mediaeval Church rejected metamorphosis as a fact, and ascribed its seeming occurrence to delusions induced by demons. In the tenth-century document known as the *Canon Episcopi*, which afterwards became part of Canon Law, it was clearly stated that whosoever believed that any man could turn, or be turned, into a creature of another species was no better than an infidel, since only God could change that which He had created. By the beginning of the fourteenth century, the force of this Canon had been weakened by the argument that it referred only to times past, and not to the new sect of witches, which was supposed to have arisen. Nevertheless, most scholars, with a few exceptions such as Jean Bodin and Henri Boguet, continued to think that any real change of nature or form was impossible, and that those who believed themselves to be lycanthropes were either lunatics whose madness was caused by Satan's direct action or by unguents supplied by him, or else were deceived by diabolical fantasies. 'The Demon', wrote Nicholas Remy in the sixteenth century, 'can so confuse the imagination of a man that he believes himself to be changed; and then the man behaves and conducts himself not as a man, but as that beast which he fancies himself to be.'[15] Some accused witches confessed that they had become wild beasts by the aid of Satan, and had done as wild beasts do, destroying sheep and cattle and even eating human flesh. Even in the height of the witch-mania, there were judges who recognised the element of insanity in such confessions; but that was not much help to the accused, since only those who had willingly opened their minds to demonic notions were thought likely to fall so deeply into the power of the Devil.

Most ordinary people in the Middle Ages accepted the fact of shape-shifting without difficulty. Giraldus Cambrensis tells an interesting story in his *Topographica Cambrensis* (*c.* 1188) concerning a priest who was travelling in Ireland, in the diocese of Ossory. He encountered a wolf which addressed him in human speech, and begged him to come and shrive his dying wife. The animal explained that long ago St Natalis had cursed the people of Ossory so that, two by two, they were forced to become wolves for seven years at a time. He and his wife were the current victims of the curse, and now the unhappy woman was dying in her wolf-form without the aid of the Church, unless the priest would consent to go to the place where she lay and shrive her. In his *Otia Imperialia* (*c.* 1211), Gervase of Tilbury records that: 'In England we often see men changed into wolves at the changes of the moon, which kind of men the French call *gerulfos*, but the English *werewulf*.' He adds that if such a wer-animal was wounded, the wound would be reproduced in the body of the human being concerned, and injuries of this sort were often used in evidence against people suspected of shape-shifting. 'Women', he says, 'have been seen and wounded in the shape of cats by persons who were secretly on the watch and . . . the next day the women have shown wounds and loss of limbs.' Five centuries later, the same idea appeared in the course of an enquiry held at Caithness in 1718. William Montgomery, a mason, declared that he was tormented and kept awake at night by the constant yowlings of cats, whom he believed to be witches. One night, unable to bear it any longer, he rushed out of his house, armed with a sword and a hatchet, and laid about him fiercely, killing two of the unfortunate cats, and wounding several others. Next day, two local women were found to have died very suddenly, and another, Margaret Nin-Gilbert, had so deep a hatchet-wound in one of her legs that the limb was virtually severed from the trunk, and eventually withered and dropped off.

Witches were still credited with the power of changing their bodily forms at will long after the general belief in shape-shifting had more or less disappeared. Mostly they were thought to become hares, or cats. Wolves became extinct comparatively early in England, thanks to the firm policies of successive kings, and as the real animals gradually vanished from the contemporary scene, so less and less was heard of werewolves. But witches continued to run (or so most people believed) as hares, or cats, as dogs, or some other animals, the first being the commonest forms. 'In good sooth, I may tell it to you as my friend,' said one of the characters in George Giffard's *Dialogue concerning Witches . . .* (1593), 'when I go but into my closes, I am afraid, for I see now and then a Hare; which my conscience giveth me is a witch, or some witch's spirit, she stareth so upon me. And sometimes I see an ugly weasel run through my yard, and there is a foul great cat sometimes in my Barn, which I have no liking unto.'[16]

In 1612, a fourteen-year-old girl of Salmesbury named Grace Sowerbutts maliciously accused her grandmother, her aunt, and a woman called Jane Southworth, of witchcraft. She declared, amongst a variety of charges, that they sometimes went about in the form of black dogs, a bodily change made possible in this case by the use of an ointment made from the bones of Thomas Walshman's child, which they had kidnapped and murdered. She also accused them of cannibalism, in that they cooked and ate the child's flesh, inviting Grace to share their meal, which she refused to do. Eventually, the whole of her wild story was proved to be a baseless fabrication, the ugly fruit of a family quarrel founded upon religious differences. The case against the three women was dismissed.

When Julian Cox was tried at Taunton in 1663, one of the witnesses stated that, being out hunting one day, he started a hare near the prisoner's house, and pursued it for some distance, until it took refuge in a great bush. There, seeing the creature was almost exhausted, and wishing to save it from his hounds, he ran round to the other side of the bush, and managed to seize it in his hands. To his amazement and terror, it immediately changed into a woman, who proved to be Julian Cox. 'He knowing her was so affrighted that his Hair stood on end; and yet spake to her and ask'd her what brought her there; but she was so far out of Breath that she could not make him any Answer.'[17] This was the end of his day's hunting, for his hounds were as terrified as he was; it was also the end of the wretched Julian Cox's adventures, and of her liberty, since at the conclusion of her trial she was convicted of witchcraft (though not on this evidence alone).

Variants of this tale of witches turning into hares, and being hunted when in that form were to be heard over and over again in the following two centuries. In her *Traditions of Devonshire* (1838), Mrs Bray relates a story current in her time concerning a Tavistock woman who turned her powers of transformation to good account. Her grandson used to get money from the neighbouring huntsmen by telling them where they could find a hare. It was noticed that he was always right, but that the quarry always got away in the end. One day, however, it was very hard pressed, and the boy was heard to cry out, 'Run, granny, run for your life!' The hare dashed into his grandmother's cottage, but when the huntsmen reached the house, they found no animal therein, but only a woman, scratched and bleeding, and panting as though she had run a long way at full speed over very rough ground.

The old belief, mentioned by Gervase of Tilbury in the twelfth century, that wounds inflicted upon a wer-animal would be reproduced in a corresponding part of the lycanthropist's body, was still current 600 years later. Many tales were told in the nineteenth century concerning a hunted hare which got away, but not before it had been bitten by one of the hounds; and the next day, some local woman was found to be suffering from an injury, never very clearly explained, which resembled that which the hare had suffered. It was, however, generally supposed to be useless to go hunting for witch-hares, or any other wer-beasts in the district, with a gun loaded only with ordinary lead bullets. Only a silver bullet, specially prepared for the purpose, was any use at all.

4 *Maleficium*

The widespread fear and hatred of witches that existed everywhere, and at all times, for as long as the general faith in magic and sorcery lasted, sprang primarily from the universal belief in *maleficium*. For scholars and learned men, it was, no doubt, his (or her) association with Devil-worship and with heresy, with demon-familiars, and the obscene and blasphemous rites of the Sabbat, that consituted the chief horror of the witch, and for the ordinary people, too, stories of such things must have added greatly to the terrors of those who heard them. But they did not create those terrors in the beginning. It was the deep-seated dread of *maleficium,* of that constant secret malice of magicians and of the occult knowledge that made that malice effective, which lay at the root of the general detestation of witches, and ensured popular support for all the laws and edicts devised at different times by ecclesiastical or civil authorities. Such laws, in all their brutal cruelty, could never have lasted as long as they did, or achieved the Statute Book at all, without the ardent approval of simple folk everywhere; and that approval was given, not so much because the witch was an anti-Christian, or in pre-Christian times, an anti-social figure, as because, by so doing, men felt they were helping to protect themselves against a danger that was uncertain, material, and never far away.

Everyone was convinced that witches could, at any time, do untold harm to all and sundry. They were blamed for storms and floods, for outbreaks of pestilence amongst human beings, and of murrain amongst cattle. They afflicted young and old with mysterious diseases, and, upon occasion, sent men mad. They blighted the crops, caused houses to catch fire, made women barren and men impotent, parted friends and lovers, and at the same time extended their malice to such small matters as preventing the butter from 'coming', or bewitching the beer. And besides all this, they were often suspected of, and sometimes confessed to, murder by image-magic, or by elfshot, by curses, spoken or written, or simply by the use of poison.

On the farm and in the dairy, the witch's power was felt in a hundred ways. If the milk yield declined, it was because the cows were overlooked, or were being magically milked from a distance by means of a rope, or straws, or the handle of an axe stuck into a wall. Sometimes a witch would come in the form of a hare and suck the cows in the field. Heanley relates that, when he was a boy, his father's garthman asked him for a crooked sixpence wherewith to shoot a witch who, he declared, had been seen round the yard in the shape of a dog. He had found two or three straws twisted round the pump-handle near the cow-byre, and was certain she had put them there to steal the milk.[1] Baring-Gould, in a footnote to Henderson's *Folklore of the Northern Counties,* cites the case of a farmer at Bratton Clovelly in the nineteenth century, who declared on oath that his milk was bewitched, and would not boil, though he put whole faggots on the fire under it. He consulted a wisewoman in Exeter, and she told him to make a fire with sticks gathered from four parishes. This he did, and as soon as the milk was set on the fire so made, it boiled over. At the same moment, the witch came to the window and looked in. She muttered something inaudible, and then withdrew, and from henceforward, the farmer was troubled no more.

To protect horses from being 'hag-ridden' by night, and cows from being overlooked, small holed pebbles known as hagstones, or witch-stones, were hung up in the stables or cow-byres, or round the animals' necks. Rowan-boughs were used for the same purpose. In Herefordshire, a young birch-tree decorated with red and white streamers and called a Maypole, was brought in on May Day and set up against the outside wall of the stable, there to remain for the rest of the year as a protection against witchcraft. A witch could stop a team of horses at his will and fix them immovably on one spot, or make them plunge and become unmanageable, unless the driver had a rowan-wood whip with him. In 1610, Katherine Lawrett, of Colne Wake in Essex, was accused at the Chelmsford Lent Sessions of employing 'certain evil and devilish arts' to bewitch a horse worth £10, which was the property of Francis Plaite, and thereby to cause its death. In 1578, Margery Stanton, of Wimbish, also in Essex, was charged at Braintree with destroying, 'of her malice aforethought', a white gelding valued at £3, and a cow worth 40s. These animals languished for four days after the spell had been laid upon them, and then died. She was more fortunate than many others accused of similar crimes, for in her case, the charge was not proven.[2]

In *A Corner of Old Cornwall* (1896), Mrs Bonham relates the story of a farmer in the Lizard district, who reproved a woman for opening a gate and allowing one of his mares to stray. It is not clear whether this woman was supposed to be a witch before this happened, but it is certain that she retorted angrily to the farmer's reproof, with the wish that none of the mare's colts would ever be reared. None was. The first was killed falling over a hedge; the next was drowned in a shallow brook; the third was kept in the stable as a precaution, but fell into a puddle of water and died because it was too weak to rise; the fourth had a crooked mouth, and starved to death. The mare had no more colts, and so the malicious intention of the woman's wish was literally fulfilled. It was probably a case of pure coincidence, following upon an outburst of bad temper; but it is easy to see how it would be likely to foster a strong local belief in witchcraft, whether the woman concerned had actually tried to overlook the mare or not.

The power of controlling the weather, especially winds and

storms, was often credited to witches. In the Middle Ages, great storms were frequently ascribed to demons, or to Satan himself, or to dragons which were seen flying through the air while the storm lasted. Such a dragon, according to Ralph Niger's *Chronicle,* was observed in 1171, sweeping over St Osyth; it was of immense size, and flying so fast that its mere passage kindled a heat great enough to burn a house, and all its outbuildings, to the ground. At Coventry, a violent wind sprang up suddenly one day in 1642, and when it sank down again, one Thomas Holt, a musician, was found dead, with his neck broken. This Holt was rumoured to have sold his soul to the Devil at some earlier date, and now, on the evening of his death-date, his neighbours remembered that they had seen a handsome stranger entering his house while the storm was raging. From this, it was widely assumed that the sudden gale had been caused by Satan coming in person on the wind to claim his own.[3]

Yet, demons and dragons notwithstanding, it was those human servants of the Devil, the witches, who were most often blamed for bad weather and high winds, and the consequences that followed them. The witches themselves believed that they had these weather-powers, or at least, they frequently confessed to calling up gales, or sudden mists, or violent rain. In 1493, Elena Dalok told the Commissary of London that 'if she bids the rain to rain, it rains at her command'.[4] Two women of Wymondham, in Norfolk, Margaret Byx and Ellen Pendleton, acknowledged in 1615 that they had taken part in a plot to burn the town. The fire was to be started by ordinary means, and was in fact kindled in the corner of a stable. Ellen Pendleton told her accomplice that it would burn the whole town next day, and to ensure that the fire could not be put out too easily, the wind should 'by conjuration' be raised to a strong gale, which would keep it going. What exactly the 'conjuration' was in this case, we do not know, but it is a fact that a gale did spring up at the relevant time, and no one seems to have doubted that the two women were responsible for it.

Sailors strongly disliked witches as a rule, though they often bought favourable winds from cunning-men and wisewomen in ports. Higden,[3] writing in the fourteenth century, mentions women in the Isle of Man who sold winds in the form of cords with three knots in them; when the first knot was loosened, a good wind arose, with the second loosening, a stronger wind, with the third, a gale. In the nineteenth century, wind-sales of this kind were still going on, not only in the Isle of Man, but in various parts of Wales and Scotland also, and in the Orkneys and Shetlands. As late as 1814, Sir Walter Scott bought a wind in Stromness from Bessie Millie, and recorded it in his diary. A whistling woman remained an object of superstitious dread amongst seafaring men almost down to our own day, because to whistle is a simple magical method of raising the wind. No skipper would allow any female to whistle on his ship; Henderson mentions a Scarborough captain in the mid-nineteenth century who would not take a young girl on board his vessel because, on another occasion, he had heard her whistle.[6]

But sailors had stronger reasons for their fear of witches than their mere association with wind. A witch's curse brought dire misfortune upon any ship, and upon the men who sailed in her. When William Tompson, a Dartmouth sailor, first went to sea after quarrelling with Alice Trevisard, who was a reputed witch, he had good reason for remembering that quarrel. He and a friend, one William Furseman, met the woman out one night and asked her what she was doing abroad so late. They were certainly rude to her, and she answered sharply. Tompson, who was probably a little the worse for drink, slipped, and she laughed at him, whereupon he struck her with his musket. She said, 'Thou shalt be better thou hadst never met with me'. Within three weeks, Tompson went to sea again. His voyage was disastrous; his ship caught fire for no ascertainable reason, and sank with the loss of nineteen lives. It is true that Tompson was saved by a Portuguese vessel, but he was carried to Spain, and imprisoned there for a year. When he came home at last, Alice Trevisard told his wife that he would soon be a prisoner again, and so he was. In less than six months, being once more at sea, he was captured by the Spaniards, and kept in prison for more than two years.

An entry for 1583 in the parish registers of Wells-next-the-Sea, in Norfolk, records the death by drowning of fourteen sailors, whose names are all given. Their deaths, it is stated,

. . . were brought to pass by the detestable working of an execrable witche of Kings Lynn, whose name was Mother

Gabley, by the boiling or rather labouring of certayn Eggs in a payle full of colde water, afterward proved sufficiently at the arraignment of ye said Witche.[7]

In 1645, Elisabeth Harris, of Faversham, confessed that she had cursed John Woodcott's boat because her son had been drowned when sailing in it, and because of that curse, it had foundered. A Cornish legend still extant ascribes the great storm of 22 October 1707, when four ships under the command of Sir Cloudesley Shovel were cast away off the Scilly Isles, and 2000 men perished, to the curse of a sailor unjustly hanged by the Admiral. There is no evidence that this man was supposed to be a witch, but the power of his curse was apparently sufficient. It is significant of the firm belief in a witch's power to harm ships that one of the confessions extorted by bullying and ill usage from the eighty-year-old John Lowes, Vicar of Brandeston, in 1645 was that he had sunk a ship by magic, apparently for no better reason than that he had happened to see it sailing by. This confession he afterwards retracted, and went to his death protesting his innocence. There seems to have been no attempt on the part of his accusers to ascertain whether any ship had in fact been wrecked at the time, and in the place mentioned, and indeed, the whole prosecution seems to have sprung originally from the malice of his parishioners, and the witch-baiting enthusiasm of the unscrupulous Matthew Hopkins.

Illnesses of every kind were ascribed to witches, including wasting diseases and fits. Victims were afflicted with sudden and unheralded pains, or with sharp bouts of fever, or made to vomit curious objects, such as pins, stones, or pieces of coal. In his *Sadducismus Triumphatus* (1689), Joseph Glanvil records that in 1658 a child at Welton vomited, in the presence of witnesses, coals and stones, some of which weighed as much as a quarter of a pound. In 1672, Magdalen Holyday, an eighteen-year-old maid-servant in the parsonage at Saxmundham, suddenly felt a pricking in her leg, like that of a large pin, and thereafter was ill for three weeks. During that time, she constantly brought up bodkins, bones, egg-shells, pieces of brass, and other small objects, and notwithstanding the treatment of two doctors, grew steadily worse. At last, however, after a violent bout of retching, she vomited a whole row of pins, very neatly stuck in a blue paper, and this apparently broke the spell. Tobias Gilbert, a cordwainer of Freston, who sent these interesting details to Richard Baxter in 1685, says that she was not troubled further, and lived to marry Sir John Hevingham's steward. According to a statement which she made to Mr Pacey, a local magistrate, she did not suspect any particular person of having betwitched her, unless it was an old woman who, shortly before her illness, had begged her for a pin and was refused it. Gilbert, whose notions were evidently somewhat puritanical, ends his letter by saying: 'Whether this punishment was inflicted by the said old woman, an emissary of Satan, or whether it was meant wholesomely to rebuke her for frequenting wakes, may-dances, and Candlemas fairs and such like pastimes, still to me remains in much doubt.[8]

In November, 1589, the celebrated Warboys case began in an odd and persistent disturbance in the house of Robert Throckmorton, of Warboys in Huntingdonshire. His eldest daughter, Jane, then aged ten, began to suffer from what appreared to be severe hysterical fits. In the course of these, she cried out that a certain Alice Samuel, a neighbour, was afflicting her. Notwithstanding this accusation, Mr Throckmorton took no action against Mrs Samuel, but called in a well-known Cambridge physician, Dr Barrow, to examine and treat the child. When the latter suggested witchcraft as the cause of her ills and asked him if he had previously suspected it, he replied that he had not. A little later, however, his four younger children became infected, as well as some of the servants, and eventually, the children's aunt, Mrs John Pickering, of the nearby village of Ellington. All accused Mrs Samuel, though there seems to have been no particular reason why they should have suspected her. The fits went on for three and a half years, during which time the Throckmorton parents showed exemplary patience in a household which must have been almost intolerable to live in. As time went on, they could scarcely avoid suspecting Mrs Samuel, but they treated her with great kindness, and at first did no more than entreat her to confess her witchcraft and remove the spell. Their leniency and forbearance form one of the most unusual features of this case, and it is possible that they were not entirely satisfied as to her guilt, in spite of the accusations continually made against her by the sufferers.

Towards the end of 1590, the wife of their landlord, Sir

Henry Cromwell, called upon the Throckmortons to sympathise with them in their troubles. This visit had unfortunate consequences for Mrs Samuel and, in contemporary opinion at least, for Lady Cromwell herself. The Samuels, like the Throckmortons, were Sir Henry's tenants, and Lady Cromwell peremptorily sent for the suspected woman. When she arrived, the children were seen to be markedly worse. Lady Cromwell roundly accused her of witchcraft, and without giving her any chance of defending herself, tore off her cap and snipped off a lock of her hair. This she gave to Mrs Throckmorton, telling her to burn it. Mrs Samuel, justifiably angered by this high-handed proceeding, said indignantly, 'Madam, why do you use me thus? I never did you any harm as yet.' The last two words were to be remembered against her later on, though no one took much notice of them at the time. That night, Lady Cromwell had alarming dreams concerning Mrs Samuel and her cat, which is perhaps not altogether surprising. Her daughter-in-law, who was sleeping with her, said afterwards that she was awakened by her cries and mutterings, and saw her moving in the bed as though she was fending off some attacker. This nightmare was the beginning of a long illness lasting fifteen months, at the end of which, in 1592, Lady Cromwell died.

In the same year, Mrs Samuel, who had recently been ill also, and was perhaps worn down by their entreaties, confessed to the Throckmortons that she had in fact bewitched their children. She promised amendment, and seemed so truly repentant that the delighted parents imagined that their troubles were at an end. But almost immediately, she retracted her confession. The children's fits continued, and Mr Throckmorton, losing patience at last, caused her to be brought before the Bishop of Lincoln and two local justices of the peace. Under their searching examination, she broke down and once more confessed herself a witch.

Meanwhile, the afflicted children came forward with a new and much more serious charge. Like everyone else, they must have heard of Lady Cromwell's death, an event which no one had hitherto connected with witchcraft. They now accused Alice Samuel of murdering her, and not alone, for they asserted that she had the willing help of John Samuel, her husband, and of Agnes, her daughter. All three were eventually sent to

Huntingdon to await the Assizes, and on 5 April 1593 they were tried and found guilty of bewitching the Throckmorton children, and of causing the death of Lady Cromwell. They were consequently hanged and, according to the law at that time, their goods, amounting to some £40, were forfeited to Sir Henry Cromwell, as Lord of the Manor. He used the money so obtained to endow an annual sermon against witchcraft, which was to be preached in Huntingdon on Lady Day by a Fellow of Queen's College, Cambridge. It was so preached until 1814, although in its later years, when opinions had changed, it was devoted chiefly to showing the impossibility rather than the wickedness of witchcraft.[9]

The witch with murderous intentions had several magical methods of killing at his or her command. A curse, spoken or written or engraved upon metal or stone tablets, was often thought to be strong enough to cause death. The same Elena Dalok who boasted in 1493 that she could control the rain also asserted that she had 'cursed very many who never lived in this world thereafter'.[10] In Cheshire, some odd figures on a cottage near Bunbury still testify to the existence of a belief in cursing-magic in the late eighteenth and early nineteenth centuries. This house, which is known as the Image House, has two small figures and some roughly-hewn stone heads on its walls. The posts which support the porch are surmounted by heads also, and there are others out in the garden. The story behind this curious ornamentation concerns a local poacher who killed a gamekeeper in a fight, and was transported for eight years. Such a sentence was then comparatively light; it was given in this case because there were some extenuating circumstances. But the poacher considered he had been wronged, and became hopelessly embittered. When he returned to England at the end of his sentence, he built the Image House on the edge of the butland, according to the old custom of 'jerry-building', which permitted a man to claim a piece of land without purchase or lease, provided he could build some sort of a house in a single night, and have the chimney smoking by sunrise. Here he lived and, since he could not reach his enemies by ordinary means, devoted himself to the more ancient form of revenge. He made and solemnly cursed the heads and figures in the names of the judge, the sheriff's officers, the witnesses, and others connected with his trial. Then he set them up on the walls and pillars of his house, and waited for the curses to take effect. It does not seem to be recorded that any of the people concerned came to a particularly evil end, but, almost certainly, every misfortune that befell them throughout their lives was ascribed to the force of the images, both by the maker, and by the majority of his neighbours.

In 1619, Margaret and Philippa Flower were tried at Lincoln for bewitching the two surviving children of the Earl of Rutland. In the course of the trial, it was revealed that, some four or five years earlier, they had also been responsible for the death of the Earl's eldest son, young Henry. The two women were both employed at Belvoir Castle, but Margaret had been dismissed for theft. To obtain her revenge, she stole one of Henry's gloves and carried it to her mother, Joan Flower, who was a reputed witch, and owned a cat named Rutterkin. This last was supposed to be her familiar. She took the glove from her daughter, stroked Rutterkin with it, and then dipped it in boiling water, pricked it several times, and buried it. The Earl's young heir fell ill and eventually died. Not content with this, the three women later attempted to prevent the Earl and Countess from having other children by stealing wool and feathers from their bed, boiling both in water mixed with blood, and rubbing them on Rutterkin's belly. They also tried the glove-magic on the two younger children, causing them severe and painful illnesses.

To all this, Margaret and Philippa confessed, and both were hanged on 11 March 1619. Their mother would doubtless have died with them but, though she was arrested, she was never tried. She refused to admit anything, and 'called for bread and butter, and wished it might neuer goe through her if she were guilty of that whereupon she was examined'. This was the old test of ordeal in one of the forms used in Anglo-Saxon times. In this case it failed; the bread choked her and she, 'mumbling it in her mouth neuer spake more words after, but fell downe and dyed as she was carried to Lincolne Jaile'.[11]

Of murder by image-magic, there are many records. This ancient and deadly form of magic provided a simple method of killing a man, and one that was comparatively safe, since the image-maker did not need to approach his dying victim, and with any luck at all could probably avoid incurring suspicion. A figure roughly resembling the person destined to die was

Joan Flower

'A figure of wax was made'

secretly made of clay or wax, or sometimes, of wood. It was given the victim's name, because his name was supposed to be an integral part of its owner's personality. Often a strand of his hair, or some nail-parings, or shreds of his clothing were added to the effigy, to give it greater power. It was pierced with nails, or pins, or thorns, and was either melted slowly before a fire, or buried in the earth. In some cases, it was laid in running water; but however it was disposed of, the effect upon its human original was the same. In all the parts where the nails or pins were driven, he suffered piercing torments in the corresponding parts of his body. If a nail was driven into the head of the image, the man went mad, if it was driven into his heart, he died instantly. Where an effigy was buried, or drowned, death was slow; as the image gradually mouldered in earth or water, so its original declined and withered, and finally died of some painful wasting disease. Nothing could save him but the timely discovery and destruction of the hidden image, or a somewhat unlikely change of heart on the part of the maker.

It was not always absolutely necessary to construct a figure of clay or wax. An existing portrait could be used instead, and indeed, almost anything could be made to represent a man symbolically, if it was magically treated in the right way. A wheatsheaf twisted into human shape and named for the victim could kill him if it was buried in the ground near his house. So could an old coat, or any other garment he had once worn, if it was secretly buried in an existing grave. In both cases, the man died a lingering death as the sheaf or the coat decayed. In 1490, Johanna Benet was charged before the Commissary of London with burning a wax candle with intent to make a man waste away as the wax melted.[12] Sometimes a living animal was used instead of an effigy, and tortured and killed in the belief that the human victim would suffer and die with it. In all these substitutions, it was not the animal, nor the candle, nor the garment, nor any other object used, that was deemed to be enchanted, but rather the human being with whom it had become magically identified.

In an Anglo-Saxon charter of about AD 963, an early example of image-magic in England is mentioned. Some land at Ailesworth in Northamptonshire was forfeited by a widow and her son because they had made an effigy of Aelsi, Wulfstan's father, and driven iron nails into it. This effigy was discovered in the woman's chamber. She was drowned at London Bridge, and her son, who was outlawed, saved his life by immediate flight.

Four centuries later, a particularly cold-blooded case of image-magic came to light in Coventry. In 1323, a magician named John de Notingham lived there, and with him lodged Robert le Mareschal, of Leicester, who also had some magical knowledge, though not as much as his landlord. On 30 November 1323, these two men were secretly approached by twenty-seven burgesses of the town, who came to propose a rather unusual bargain with them. They were all highly respectable men, whose names we know, and in some cases, their trades also, since they were preserved in a statement later made by Robert le Mareschal. Nevertheless, the first thing they did on arrival at the house was to swear John and Robert to secrecy, and then proceed quite calmly to propose a course of action involving witchcraft, murder, and high treason.

They declared that 'they could not live for the harsh treatment that the prior of Coventry had accorded them, and did, from one day to the next, and for the support which our lord the King monsieur Despencer, Earl of Winchester, and monsieur Hugh Despencer, the son, gave the said prior, to their destruction, and that of the town of Coventry.' They now asked that John de Notingham should, 'by his necromancy and arts', destroy the King and the Prior, the two Despencers, and also the seneschal and the cellarer of the priory. In return, they offered him £20, and his maintenance in any religious house of his choice, and Robert would receive £15 for helping him.

The two magicians agreed. Part of the promised money was paid over on account, and seven pounds of wax and two ells of canvas were supplied by the burgesses for the making of the images. John and Robert retired to an old house just outside the town, and set to work. By the end of April, 1324, they had made six images, one for each of the persons named by the burgesses. They had also made a seventh, which was to be used for experimental purposes. For this, they chose as their subject a man named Richard de Sowe, not because they disliked him, or had anything against him, but simply because he happened to live nearby. At about midnight on 27 April, John gave his accomplice a sharp spit of lead, and told him to run it into the forehead of Richard's effigy. Next morning, when Robert went round to Richard's house to see what had happened, he found the wretched man quite mad and raving, unable to recognise anybody, and continually shrieking out 'Harrow!'. In this state he remained until 20 May, when the leaden spit was pulled out of the head and thrust into the heart of the image. Within a few days, de Sowe was dead.

By this horrible experiment, it was made clear that the magicians' work was completely successful. All that remained to do was to use the other six images for the murderous purpose for which they had been made. But before that could be done, Robert le Mareschal seems to have lost his nerve. It is probable that questions were beginning to be asked about the curious death of Richard de Sowe, and perhaps rumour was connecting it too closely with the lonely house in a field half a league from Coventry. At all events, Robert made a statement before the Coroner and 'appealed', that is, accused, John de Notingham and the burgesses of the felony in which he had himself played so active a part. By thus adopting the mediaeval equivalent of turning king's evidence, he sought to escape from what he feared was inevitable and dire punishment. The case was tried in 1325, but by that time John de Notingham had died in prison. The burgesses were all acquitted, though it is not very easy to see why, since they were the main instigators of the whole affair. As for Robert le Mareschal, he was still in prison when the trial ended, but what became of him afterwards is not recorded.[13]

It was commonly believed that if an image made with evil intent could be discovered and destroyed in time, the individual concerned would recover. But there were, apparently, exceptions to this rule. In April 1594, the Earl of Derby fell ill at Latham. At first, his trouble was thought to be purely natural, caused, as his physicians supposed, by a surfeit combined with too much violent exercise in Easter week. On 10 April however, about midnight, one, Master Halsall, a member of the Earl's household, discovered a waxen image concealed in the bedroom. It had, as Stow tells us in his *Annales*, 'hair like unto the hair of his honour's head, twisted through the belly thereof, from the navel to the secrets', and it was also marked with spots, exactly like those which appeared next day on the patient's stomach and sides. The horrified Master Halsall at once burnt the effigy, in the hope that, by so doing, he would break the spell and save his Lord; but says Stow, 'it fell out contrary to his love and affection, for after the melting thereof, he more and more declined'.

A woman of about fifty years old, who appears to have been a local wisewoman, seems to have tried to save the Earl by her own charms and potions, and did, apparently, succeed in easing him on several occasions; but one of the doctors, becoming suspicious, prevented her from continuing. Although the image had been destroyed as soon as it was found, the Earl remained convinced that he lay under the power of enchantment, and constantly 'cried out that the Doctors laboured in vain, because he was certainly bewitched'.[14] And being thus firmly assured of approaching death, he died on 16 April, six days after the finding of the effigy.

Faith in the efficacy of image-magic lasted a very long time, and is perhaps not altogether extinct even yet. The *corps creadh,* or figure made of clay, and either pin-studded, or set in a running stream, was well-known in Scotland all through last century. When the offices of the Hereford Rural District Council were being repainted in 1960, an eighteenth-century doll was found hidden in an alcove in the cellar. It wore a long, full-skirted dress, and a cap on its head. Attached to the skirt was a piece of paper on which was written the name Mary Ann Wand, and the words: 'I act this spell upon you from my whole heart, wishing you to never rest nor eat nor sleep the restern part of your life. I hope your flesh will waste away and I hope you will never spend another penny I ought to have. Wishing this from my whole heart.'[15] Nothing is now remembered about Mary Ann Wand and her enemy, but here, apparently, we have a surviving relic of image-magic as it was known in eighteenth-century Hereford.

In 1843, during an action for assault the Norwich magistrates heard in evidence that a certain Mrs Bell had injured a man named Curtis by candle-magic. Mrs Curtis stated that she had seen her light a candle, stick pins in it, and then put dragons-blood and water, and some of her own nail-parings into an oyster-shell. This she put on the fire, and repeated some words over it. As soon as she had done so, Mr Curtis' arms and legs were 'set fast', and he was unable to move. This seems to be much the same spell as that of which Johanna Benet was accused in 1490, except that she intended the death of her victim, and apparently, Mrs Bell did not.[16] *The New York Times* for 14 December 1900 reported that a pin-studded effigy of President McKinley had been burnt, by an Italian with a grievance, on the steps of the American Embassy in London. And nearer our own day, there was in a witch-museum in Gloucestershire (now gone from there), an effigy of a W.A.A.F. officer from the last war. It was a figure dressed in the uniform of such an officer, and it had a long pin driven right through one of its eyes. It was not at all a pleasant sight.

Hopkins with a suspected witch

5 The Discovery of Witches

When the witch-mania was at its height in England, most simple people – and many who would not have thought of themselves thus – tended to ascribe every illness or misfortune, slight or serious, that befell them to the action of witches. Given a sincere belief in *maleficium,* this was a natural, and even a reasonable thing to assume; and in the case of relatively minor ills, it was often easier and more convenient to blame witchcraft than to admit one's own fault or carelessness as the cause. The identification of the guilty party was not always quite so simple. If there was a known witch in the district, he or she would, of course, be the first to be suspected. So too, if threats uttered by one party to a violent quarrel were followed too quickly by misfortunes to the other party which seemed to fulfil those threats, or a local wisewoman or cunning-man, being consulted, mentioned a name, or by using a traditional charm, forced the guilty person to betray himself. But often there was no such obvious suspect available, and then it was that men and women began to look nervously round among their neighbours, and wonder which of these seemingly innocent persons was a hidden witch.

There was usually nothing to distinguish a witch at first sight from those amongst whom he or she lived. It is true that any one who was badly deformed, or was exceptionally ill-favoured, who squinted or was 'trough-eyed',* or physically peculiar in any way, was liable to be looked at askance, and so was any individual who was more than usually foul-mouthed, or seemed by nature unduly quarrelsome and unfriendly. Yet some who had none of these characteristics might turn out to have an unexpected knowledge of magic, so that an ordinary man could never be quite certain who was or was not a witch. The usual modern conception of a malevolent witch is an old, decrepit woman, living alone in poverty, shunned by her neighbours, and having only a cat or a toad for companion. That some, perhaps many, were in fact like that, we know from the details of the witch-trials, or from the accounts of contemporary writers. In 1584, Reginald Scot wrote of one sort of women 'said to be witches', who were 'commonly old, lame, blear-eyed, pale, foul, and full of wrinkles', and added that they were 'poor, sullen, superstitious, and Papists'.[1] Sixty-three years later, the Reverend John Gaule, Vicar of Great Staughton in Huntingdonshire, recorded (with indignation) how

> every old woman with a wrinkled face, a furr'd brow, a hairy lip, a gobber tooth, a squint eye, a squeaking voice, or a scolding tongue, having a rugged coat on her back, a skull-cap on her head, a spindle in her hand, and a Dog or Cat by her side, is not only suspected but pronounced for a witch.[2]

But this was not the whole picture. Many alleged witches were no more than middle-aged, and some not so much, nor were they all either women, or destitute. Male practitioners of magic were commonly thought to be far fewer in number than female ones, but they existed nevertheless, and to be a man was no automatic protection against the suspicions of one's neighbours. In an atmosphere so uncertain, hardly any one was

*Having one eye considerably lower than the other.

altogether safe. It would not, of course, be right to believe that,
even in the worst days of the terror, men and women went
about in constant dread of being overlooked, or having some
horrifying spell cast upon them. Witchcraft was widely feared,
but cases of it did not occur every day, and there must have
been many people who lived all their lives without ever coming
into contact with any thing of the kind. Yet the old dread was
never far away, and it took very little to rouse it, with all the
bitter suspicion, cruelty, and outbursts of violence that very
often followed.

A suspected person was liable to be scratched 'above the
breath' in order to break a spell by drawing blood, hustled to the
nearest pond and made to undergo the swimming test, and
almost certainly roughly handled on his way to the house of the
local justice. There the conduct of the affair passed from the
people into the hands of the Law. Sometimes the effects of
sudden panic carried the accusers too far, and the alleged witch
perished before he or she could be formally charged. Such cases
were fortunately rare. In 1643, a party of Parliamentary soldiers, with their officers, were passing through Newbury, in
Berkshire, when one of them saw a woman apparently walking
on the water of the River Kennet, 'with as much ease and
firmness as if one should walk or trample on the earth . . .'. It
seems that some local woman was crossing the river on a plank,
or some sort of raft, but the credulous soldiers at once made up
their minds that here was witchcraft. When she landed, they
saw quite clearly the board she had used for her passage, but
they seized her all the same, demanding to know who she was,
and dragging her before their officers. The latter, as credulous
as their men, first questioned her and then, getting no answers
from her, ordered her to be shot.

This proved to be rather less easy than the soldiers expected.
Two of the best marksmen apparently missed their aim.
Another set his carbine close to her breast, 'where discharging,
the bullet back rebounded like a ball, and narrowly he missed it
in his face that was the shooter'. A third man attacked her with
a sword, but according to a contemporary account,[3] it was not
until one soldier proposed 'scoring above the breath' that the
witch's powers of resistance suddenly failed, and she was killed
by a pistol discharged under her ear. We do not know the name

of this poor creature, who is usually called simply 'the Witch of Newbury', nor is there any evidence whatever to show that she was, in fact, a witch; but the unreasonable terror apparently shared by men and officers alike was enough to bring about the unfortunate woman's murder.

An even sadder story is told of a Wiltshire woman at about the same period. From an account written in 1685-6, and reproduced in the *Gentleman's Magazine,* 1832, we learn that

> Alice Elger, widow, dwelling in Westport, became so audaciously noxious to the good inhabitance, there being none but martial law then, it was about 1643; Malmesbury being then in the hands of the Armies ranged against the King; that the Soldiers and some of the lowest of the people did in the mercat place use her very roughly, moved by an instant emergent, so that she, perhaps to avoid the like, went home and poisoned herself, as was then believed, and was buried in cross way as a felon of herself.

Certain signs were commonly looked for in a suspected witch, and various tests (most of them of very doubtful legality), were used to determine guilt or innocence. It was generally believed that a witch could not weep, though in fact some actually did so at their trials or preliminary examinations, and this is recorded in the contemporary accounts of the proceedings. It was also supposed that no witch could recite the whole of the Lord's Prayer on demand, but would almost certainly break down before the end, usually at the words 'lead us not into temptation'. An odd but quite widespread notion was that, if a suspect was weighed against the Church Bible and proved to be lighter than the book, it was a sign of guilt. In 1759, Susannah Haynokes, of Wingrave, near Aylesbury, was accused of bewitching a neighbour's spinning-wheel, and her husband insisted on her being tried by the time-honoured Church Bible method. Accordingly, she was weighed against the book, 'when to the no small mortification of her accuser, she out-weighed it, and was honourably acquitted of the charge'.[4] As late as 1780, the *Morning Post* for 28 January of that year reported that two women of Bexhill being suspected of witchcraft, the inhabitants of that town went to the local clergyman and demanded that they should be either swum or weighed. He chose the less cruel of the two tests and had them weighed, one after the other, with the result that, proving heavier than the Bible, both were cleared in the eyes of their neighbours.

Marks of various kinds on the bodies of suspected persons were frequently taken to be signs of guilt. Old scars, cysts, moles, warts, or natural excrescences were given a diabolical meaning, and any unusual swelling or protuberance was thought to provide evidence of the feeding of familiars. The Devil's mark, by which Satan identified his own, might be discovered on any part of the body, but was rarely easily found. It was, said Michael Dalton,[5]

> ... sometimes like a blue spot or a red spot, like a flea-biting; sometimes the flesh sunk in and hollow (all which for a time may be covered, yea taken away, but will come again, to their old form). And these Devils marks be insensible, and being pricked will not bleed, and be often in their secretest parts, and therefore require diligent and careful search.

Such 'diligent and careful search' meant in effect a minute and humiliating examination carried out in public, usually by searchers appointed for the purpose by the justice concerned, but sometimes by an angry and excited mob of accusers too impatient to wait for the slow course of Law. Because the Devil's mark was supposed to be insensitive, any suspicious spot or area was liable to be tested with a pin or some other sharp instrument. If the place pricked proved to be callous, or no blood flowed when the pin was withdrawn, its diabolical cause, and consequently the accused person's guilt, was immediately assumed.

Sometimes a professional pricker or witch-finder would be summoned by a town council or a guild, or by some anxious minister, to examine the suspected witches in the locality. In his *England's Grievance in Relation to the Coal Trade* (1655), Ralph Gardiner described the visit of such a man to Newcastle-on-Tyne in 1649. The town council had decided to send for a Scottish pricker who had made a name for himself in his own country. He was to be paid twenty shillings for every witch unmasked, and was to have his travelling expenses from Scotland refunded. The townspeople were invited to co-operate by lodging complaints against any person whom they suspected. 'The magistrates', said Gardiner,

sent their bellman through the town, ringing his bell, and crying, all people that would bring any complaint against any woman for a witch, they should be sent for, and tryed by the person appointed

As a result of this announcement,

Thirty women were brought into the town-hall, and stript, and then openly had pins thrust into their bodies, and most of them was found guilty, near twenty seven of them by him and set aside.

However, a certain Lieutenant-Colonel Hobson, who was present, was not altogether satisfied with the proceedings. The witch-finder told him that he could tell whether a woman was a witch or not by her looks. Nevertheless,

when the said person was searching of a personable and good-like woman, the said colonel replied, and said, surely this woman is none, and need not be tried, but the scotch-man said she was, for the town said she was, and therefore he would try her; and presently in the sight of all the people, laid her body naked to the waist, with her clothes over her head, by which fright and shame, all her blood contracted into one part of her body, and then he ran a pin into her thigh, and then suddenly let her coats fall, and then demanded whether she had nothing of his in her body, but did not bleed, but she being amazed, replied little, then he put his hand up her coats and pulled out the pin, and set her aside as a guilty person, and child of the devil, and fell to try others whom he made guilty.

Lieutenant colonel Hobson, perceiving the alteration of the foresaid woman, by her blood settling in her right parts, caused that woman to be brought again, and her clothes pulled up to her thigh, and required the scot to run the pin into the same place, and then it gushed out of blood, and the said scot cleared her, and said she was not a child of the devil.

How many others might have been saved, had the observant eye of Colonel Hobson been upon them during their examination, we cannot tell now. This particular pricker was eventually hanged in Scotland, and not before it was time, since by his own confession, he had been responsible for the deaths of no less than 220 women, for each of whom he had been paid 20s.

Swimming, or floating, a suspect was a well-known test for witchcraft. It was a descendant of the ancient ordeal by water, which existed in northern Europe before the advent of Christianity. When the latter religion was adopted by the different countries, including our own, the people carried the notion of ordeal with them, substituting an appeal to Christ for the older appeal to Woden. In Anglo-Saxon times, and onwards until the early thirteenth century, there were four forms of ordeal, used mainly in cases of theft, homicide, adultery, and witchcraft. One, the simplest, was the ordeal by bread, in which the accused person attempted to swallow bread, or a specially made cake, and was expected to choke upon it if he was guilty. The great Earl Godwin is said to have died thus in 1053 when he swore that he had had no hand in the murder of Edward the Confessor's brother, Alfred. There were two ordeals by fire, in one of which the person concerned had to thrust his hand into boiling water and draw up a stone from the bottom of the vessel containing it. In the other, he was expected to carry, or to walk over, red hot iron rods. The scalds or burns incurred thus had to heal completely within a stated (and very short) time in order to prove innocence. In the water-ordeal, the individual to be tested was bound hand and foot, and a rope was tied round his waist, so that he could be saved from drowning if he was in danger of it. He was then thrown into the water where, if he was innocent, it was supposed that he would sink; but if he floated, he was clearly guilty.

In its heyday, ordeal was a religious as well as a judicial ceremony. By it, God was implored to show, by a sign, where the truth lay, and those to whom that sign was all-important had to prepare themselves to receive it by prayer and fasting and confession. The whole ritual was governed by strict rules intended to protect the accused person, and the sanction of the civil and ecclesiastical authorities were necessary for its legal performance. If it was carried through without such sanctions, those concerned were liable to heavy fines. Thus, in 1185, the town of Preston, in Lancashire, was fined five marks for submitting a man to ordeal without any such official warranty.

In 1219, both the fire- and the water-ordeal were abolished in

England by Henry III, in deference to the opinion of the Church which had come to regard the custom as superstitious. They ceased, therefore, to be legal, but the water-test seems to have continued illegally for a long time thereafter. It was probably much easier, in the case of a dispute, or of strong suspicion, to have recourse to the nearest pond rather than to the courts. It lost its religious character, of course, since priests no longer took part in it, but rough and ready though it became, it never quite died out because the country-folk believed in its efficacy. In the late sixteenth century, it received great encouragement from King James I who, in his *Daemonologie* (1597), declared that 'fleeting on the water' was one of the best ways of finding out witches because the pure water would not receive those who had 'shaken off them the sacred Water of Baptism, and wilfully refuse the benefit thereof'. Throughout the following century, the old swimming-test, though still illegal, was widely used. The magistrates who ought to have forbidden it usually ignored, or winked at it; some were even present when it took place, and in 1645 Margaret Bruff and Anne Howsell were swum at Rye by the direct order of the Mayor.[6]

Swimming was never without its opponents. Some disliked it because it was an illegal practice, others because it was cruel and brutal, and seemed to them very unreliable as a test. Not every one believed that any person who floated during the process was necessarily guilty. 'They swam him at Framlingham', wrote John Rivett to Francis Hutchinson, concerning the treatment and death of old John Lowes in 1645, 'but that was no true Rule to try him by; for they put in honest People at the same Time, and they swam as well as he'.[7] Most people who were forced to undergo the test did their absolute best to sink, because, if they floated, they were either declared guilty then and there, or were ducked again at a later date. The Widow Comon, suspected of witchcraft, was thrown into the river at Coggeshall on 13 July 1699. She swam, so she was given what her accusers doubtless regarded as 'a second chance', and thrown in again on 19 July. Once more, she floated. A third attempt was made on 24 July, but, as John Bufton records in his Diary,[8] 'she swam and did not sink'. This might have been considered sure proof of guilt, and probably was, but rather curiously, she does not appear to have been committed for trial, or suffered any other penalty. She died nevertheless, in the following December, perhaps as a result of the shock and terror of her three duckings. In 1717, when depositions were made at the Autumn Assizes in Leicester against Jane Clarke, of Great Wigston, her son, and her daughter, witnesses stated that all three had been publicly swum, having their thumbs and great toes tied together, and that being thrown thus bound into the water, 'they swam like a cork, a piece of paper, or an empty Barrel, tho' they strove all they could to sink'.[9] Though they could not know it then, these three had the distinction of being the last people to be committed for witchcraft in this country. They were not in fact tried, for the Grand Jury threw out the Bill.

The most deplorable by-product of the general witch-fear was the rise of the professional witch-finders. These were men who claimed to have studied the whole question of witchcraft very carefully, and to have greater experience in the detection of witches than any ordinary citizens. In fact, few of them showed any special knowledge, relying mainly on traditional tests, and not always troubling to carry through these very thoroughly, as was seen in the Newcastle case already mentioned. They flourished chiefly in Scotland, but some were also found in England during the worst period of the persecution. Theirs was an easy and lucrative trade, travelling from town to town on the invitation of some council or minister, and profiting by the hysteria of the inhabitants. They were paid for all the witches detected, and treated with a kind of nervous respect by the people who saw them at their work. When some wretched individual had been declared guilty by the witch-finder, the latter's responsibility, ceased, unless he was called as a witness at the subsequent trial. Normally, he came to the place concerned, swam, pricked, or bullied the suspects brought before him, set a number aside as witches, and then took his blood-money and departed. The accused were handed to the courts for trial, and if, as sometimes, though rarely, happened, one, or more, was subsequently proved innocent, no punishment for false testimony was visited upon the witch-finder. James Balfour, of Gorhous, after a long and active career as a pricker, was forbidden to practise by the Privy Council in 1632 on the grounds that his knowledge had 'only been conjectural', but no penalty other than the loss of income involved seems to have been inflicted upon him.[10] When the tide of public opinion finally turned against the witch-finders, a few were imprisoned, and one at least was hanged, as has already been noticed, but the majority simply retired into private life, and were heard of no more.

Witch-finders were not officially recognised in English law, though town councils and similar bodies were often responsible for bringing them into a particular district. In 1579, Samuel Cocwra was licensed by the Privy Council to search for conjurors in the counties of Salop, Worcester and Montgomery. Much later, when Matthew Hopkins was travelling through the Eastern and adjacent counties, calling himself the Witch-Finder General, there were many who believed that he had been given a special commission by Parliament to track down witches, but in fact, there is no evidence that he ever possessed anything of the sort. In Scotland, pricking was a recognised procedure, but even here there were occasional complaints of unauthorised persons who went about terrorising the countryside without warrant or licence. One such was Alexander Chisholm of Commer who was charged in 1662 with imprisoning suspects in his own house, and there treating them so barbarously that 'one of them hath become distracted, another by cruelty is departed this life, and all of them have confessed whatever they were pleased to demand of them, all of which is done against his Majesty's laws and authority, they being free subjects'.[11] The local minister, and some others, were charged at the same time with having known all about these illegal activities while they were going on, and conniving at them. Brutal as the whole detestable trade was, few witch-finders either tried or were allowed, to go as far as Chisholm; but the very nature of the tests commonly used, and the apparent absence of any regulations restraining the practitioner's actions, must inevitably have created strong temptations to cruelty which few, if any, could resist altogether.

The most notorious English witch-finder was Matthew Hopkins who, with his assistant, John Stearne, pursued a comparatively brief but none the less deadly career in Essex, East Anglia, and the adjoining regions between 1644 and 1646. Hopkins is said to have been the son of a Puritan minister at Wenham, in Suffolk, and to have practised for some time as a lawyer in Ipswich. Eventually he moved to Manningtree, in Essex, where, according to his own account, he was first attracted to the work of witch-finding by noticing the activities of certain witches there. In his *Discovery of Witches* (written two years later to defend himself against the growing opposition aroused by his methods), he related how, in March, 1644, he discovered that 'some seven or eight of that horrible sect of Witches living in the Town where he lived' were accustomed to meet near his house every six weeks, '(being always on the Friday night)' and during this meeting, 'had their several solemn sacrifices offered to the Devil'. He also alleged that four of these witches, moved by hatred, had sent the Devil in the form of a bear to kill him in his own garden. No harm seems to have befallen him as a result of this; but plenty of harm befell the four women concerned, for they were among the nineteen unfortunates who were hanged for witchcraft after the Chelmsford Assizes in July 1645.[12]

Besides pricking or swimming the suspects, Hopkins often kept them without sleep or rest all through the night, or several nights together, deprived them of food, and otherwise ill-treated them. In this way, he obtained some very remarkable confessions. His first victim was Elisabeth Clarke, of Manningtree, who, after being kept awake for three nights on end, confessed her guilt, acknowledged that she possessed five imps, and called them into the room, where ten people were assembled to watch her. These imps all had very peculiar names, and each one had some faint, but distinct, resemblance to a small domestic animal. However, the ten witnesses, (including Hopkins himself), were apparently satisfied that they were indeed imps of Hell.

So too, when he was in Suffolk a little later, Hopkins forced a confession from an old Royalist clergyman, John Lowes, who had been Vicar of Brandeston for nearly fifty years, and was eighty years of age at the time of the witch-finder's visit. The old man vehemently denied the accusations brought against him, and was swum in the moat of Framlingham Castle. He floated. Thereafter, he was kept awake for several nights, with relays of watchers to 'run him backwards and forwards about the Room until he was out of Breath. Then they rested him a little, and then ran him again: And thus they did for several Days and Nights together, till he was weary of his Life, and was scarce sensible of what he said or did'.[13] In the end, the unhappy clergyman broke down and confessed to a remarkable number of crimes, including keeping and feeding familiars, making a covenant with Satan, destroying cattle, and sinking a ship which he happened to see sailing by when he was walking near the sea. It is true that he retracted his confessions as soon as he had recovered from the ill-treatment he had received, and once more asserted his complete innocence; but that could not save him. He was tried at Bury St Edmunds, along with seventeen others, condemned, and duly executed at the end of August 1645. He wished for the Anglican burial service to be read over him when he was dead, but this grace being denied to him, he read the service himself while he was being driven to the gallows.

Hopkins and Stearne, together or separately, travelled through Suffolk, Norfolk, Bedfordshire, Huntingdonshire, and Northamptonshire as well as Essex, and during their wanderings they were responsible for the deaths of a very large number of witches, mostly women. It was certainly not less than two hundred, and was probably many more. Eventually, however, the brutality of Hopkins' methods, and the cost of his visits, aroused a good deal of local opposition. In April 1646, John Gaule, the Vicar of Great Staughton, in Huntingdonshire, preached so vehement a sermon against witch-finders that Hopkins, though he visited several other places in Huntingdonshire, did not dare to go to Great Staughton. He also met with hostility in Bedfordshire, and certain very awkward questions put to him through the Norfolk Assize judges forced him to publish his *Discovery of Witches* in self-defence. This appeared in 1647, and a year later Stearne also found it necessary to defend himself in his *Confirmation and Discovery of Witchcraft*. By the time this book appeared, Hopkins had died of consumption, and Stearne himself had retired from his dreadful profession. Witch-finding as a career persisted for some time in England after these two had ceased to practise, but the heart had already gone out of it, and, finally, the strength of the local opposition everywhere made it too difficult for any would-be witch-finder. The day of the ruthless and mercenary scoundrels who lived by destroying others was nearing its sunset when Hopkins died; and English air was the purer for it.

6   Fraud and Malice

The great majority of witchcraft accusations were honestly made, however coloured by terror and ignorance they might be. The informer laid his charge before the magistrate in the first instance because he believed it to be true and usually he had no other intention than to protect himself and his neighbours from evil magic, and to see the guilty person punished. Nor were his accusations always entirely without foundation. Because alleged witches were so often accused of obviously impossible acts, we tend today to forget that many of them really were criminals, both in intention and in fact. Magic cut across the ordinary lines of human thought and action, and those who practised it strayed easily beyond the confines of the law. They were often involved in illegal conspiracies, sometimes as instigators, sometimes as accomplices. They made images for murder, and when these failed, they sometimes resorted to poison, which did not fail. At all times, they were peculiarly susceptible to the temptation of using their powers as a sort of spiritual blackmail, whereby they could attain their own ends. Magistrates and people alike believed that, in putting down sorcery, they were stamping out a detestable and unnatural crime, and they had a certain amount of justification for their belief. Some of their methods now appear to us almost as horrible as the alleged offence, but the fact remains that justice and accuser alike were usually sincere in their intentions, and were trying to do their duty as they saw it.

There were, however, cases where the accuser's part was not quite so innocent. With a crime so nebulous and so difficult to disprove by ordinary means, the opportunities for malicious and fraudulent accusations were immense. To accuse an enemy of witchcraft was an easy method of revenge; to declare oneself bewitched was a short cut to that flattering attention so much desired by unbalanced and hysterical individuals. Charges shown to be deliberately untruthful occur in the records of numerous witch-trials, and it is certain that there were many more, of which we now know nothing.

A strong tradition exists in Lancashire that Alice Nutter, of Rough Lee, perished in 1612 as the result of a conspiracy. She was accused of foregathering with the witches of Pendle Forest, of being present at the Good Friday gathering at Malkin Tower, and of helping to bring about the death of Henry Mitton by magic. She confessed nothing, and even in that age of ready suspicion and easy belief, her alleged association with the other witches amazed everyone who knew her. They were poor and illiterate people, mostly the members and friends of two local families. She was, according to Thomas Potts, 'a rich woman; had a great estate, and children of good hope; in the common opinion of the world, of good temper, free from envy and malice'. Potts was present at her trial, as clerk to Sir Edward Bromley, and was quite evidently at a loss to explain how she became involved in such a crime, and with such accomplices. Her position and her reputation alike made her guilt appear very unlikely at first sight; nevertheless she was convicted, and in due course, executed. Potts says that 'her own children were never able to move her to confess any particular offence, or declare anything, even in *articulo mortis:* which is a fearful thing to all that were present, who knew she was guilty.'[1]

This anxiety of her children to make their mother acknowledge herself a witch and a murderess has a somewhat sinister sound. Local tradition asserts that they had their own reasons for disliking her, and adds that the examining magistrate, Roger Nowell, conspired with James Device, one of those who gave evidence against her, because of a long-standing dispute over a boundary mark. We cannot now hope to disentangle the truth of this story, with its dark hints of a family feud stretched to the point of murder by false testimony. It is possible that Alice Nutter did dabble in magic, from motives of curiosity, or perhaps from boredom. She may have gone to secret meetings in the Forest, and have interested herself in the other activities of the local witches. Probably she had some connection with them, though it may have been only slight; and it is not impossible that, having taken the first step along the forbidden road, she may even have descended at last to the ultimate crime of magical murder. But even to her contemporaries, there seemed to be something peculiar about this case, which rested chiefly upon the evidence of James and Elisabeth Device, themselves condemned for witchcraft at the same Assizes as herself, and the too ready opinion of a magistrate known to be her enemy. She died without admitting anything, and nothing now remains to us but the record of her trial and condemnation, and the lingering local tradition of her innocence.

If she was in fact guiltless, she was not the only Lancashire woman to be wrongfully accused in the seventeenth century. Grace Sowerbutts' charges against her grandmother and two other women of Salmesbury were heard at the same 1612 Assizes, and were fortunately dismissed as the nonsense they were. In 1634, Edmund Robinson, the ten-year-old son of a mason living in Pendle Forest, came forward with a wild story about certain individuals living not far from his home. He said that when he was out on the previous All Saints' Day, he met two greyhounds in the path, and tried to make them run after a hare. They would not, and he beat them, whereupon they both changed into human beings, one a little boy whom he did not know, and the other a local woman named Frances Dicconson. She offered him a shilling if he would promise to say nothing about this encounter, but he virtuously refused the bribe. She then turned the unknown little boy into a white horse, mounted young Robinson upon it, and took him to a nearby house known as Hoarstones. There he saw a company of some threescore men and women passing in, of whom he was afterwards able to identify nineteen. A fire was burning on the hearth, and meat roasting before it; a young woman whom he did not know offered him food and drink, but after the first taste, he refused to take any more. Presently he followed some of the company into a barn where there were six ropes hanging down from the roof. On each of these, one person pulled, and milk, butter in lumps, and hot meat came streaming down, and fell into basins. When the first six people were satisfied, six more took their places, one to each rope. He also saw three women take down from the beam three 'pictures' into which many sharp thorns had been thrust. Being frightened by all these strange sights, he ran away and, according to his father, arrived home crying, and quite beside himself with terror.

This very remarkable story was repeated by him as a sworn statement to two magistrates, Richard Shuttleworth and John Starkie, on 10 February in the following year. These men, who remembered the witch-trials of 1612 in the same district, accepted it without question, and ordered about twenty arrests on the strength of it. The prisoners were heard at the Lenten Assizes in Lancaster, and seventeen were convicted. Only one of the accused confessed anything. This was Margaret Johnson, who admitted that she had made a covenant for her soul with a devil named Mamilion, who appeared to her in the form of a man wearing a black suit tied with silk points. She also agreed that there had been a gathering of witches at Hoarstones on All Saints' Day, though she herself was not present at it.

Notwithstanding this confession, and the findings of the jury the Assize judge seems to have entertained some doubts as to Edmund Robinson's trustworthiness, and managed to get the proceedings reported to the King in Council. The Bishop of Chester was asked to examine seven of the prisoners. Three of those chosen for re-examination, a man and two women, had already died in prison, but the remaining four – Frances Dicconson, Jennet Hargreaves, Margaret Johnson, and Mary Spencer – were questioned by the Bishop. He came to the conclusion that the charges against them were mainly based upon malice and sheer ignorance. He sent them to London, where they were examined by Dr Harvey, the King's physician, and other doctors, and cleared of the accusation of having witch-marks on their bodies. The King, who like his father, James I, had a great aptitude for detecting fraud, and took an interest in this case, also examined the four prisoners in person, and young Robinson as well.

The latter finally admitted that his story was entirely untrue. He was, of course, familiar with the witch-traditions of his own district, and he had heard some of the accused persons spoken of as witches, and from all this he had spun his own elaborate story, out of an exuberant imagination and a desire for mischief. No doubt there was a great deal of truth in this explanation, but it is possible that it is not the whole truth. Dr Webster, in his *Displaying of Supposed Witchcraft* (1677), says that the boy was instructed to bring these charges against certain people by his father, and others. It is perhaps significant that the first witch to be mentioned by name was Frances Dicconson, with whose husband the elder Robinson had quarrelled over the sale of a cow. Mary Spencer also complained that another witness, Nicholas Cunliffe, had been the enemy of her family for the past five or six years, and that his evidence was malicious and untrue. There is no doubt that Edmund's father encouraged him in his wild statements, and though the child may have been the first to think of accusing Frances Dicconson, it is probable that some of the details of his story, and the names of supposed witches were suggested to him by older people. At one time, he was taken about the countryside to detect witches elsewhere, and it was then that Dr Webster first met him. His account of that meeting suggests that there may have been more in the boy's tale than mere childish lying and boastfulness.

He relates how,

It came to pass that the said Boy was brought into the Church at Kildwick, a large Parish Church where I (being then Curate there) was preaching in the afternoon, and was set upon a stool to look about him, which moved some little disturbance in the congregation for a while. After prayers, I enquired what the matter was; the people told me it was the boy that discovered witches; upon which I went to the house where he was to stop all night, and here I found him and two very unlikely persons, that did conduct him and manage the business. I desired to have some discourse with the boy in private, but that they utterly refused. Then, in the presence of a great many people, I took the boy near me and said: 'Good boy, tell me truly and in earnest, didst thou see and hear such strange things at the meeting of witches as is reported by many thou didst relate?' But the two men, not giving the boy leave to answer, did pluck him from me, and said he had been examined by two *able* justices of the peace, and they *did never ask him such a question*. To whom I replied, the persons accused had therefore the more wrong. . . .

Many years before, in 1599, another boy confessed that the tale he had told three years earlier, was quite untrue. He told it, he said, 'to get myself a glory thereby'. In February 1596, Thomas Darling, of Burton-on-Trent, then aged fourteen, had gone out hare-hunting with his uncle, Robert Toone. He returned alone, and that evening he was sick. On the following day, he began to have fits, and declared that he saw green angels and a green cat. His alarmed relatives sent for the doctor, but the latter could do nothing for the lad except give it as his opinion that he was bewitched. This belief was confirmed by the fact that the convulsions became worse when certain passages from the Gospel of St John were read aloud.

Darling's story was that, after parting from his uncle, he met a strange woman in the wood, with whom he fell out, although he did not know who she was. High words passed between them, and she had threatened him. He said she wore a grey gown and a broad-brimmed hat, and had three warts on her face. From this description, the neighbours at once realised that she was one of the witches of Stapenhill, either Elisabeth Wright, or her daughter, Alse Gooderidge. It is extremely probable that young Darling knew perfectly well who she was, and had either worked himself into an hysterical state through fear of her anger, or had deliberately ascribed his fits to her because of her already established reputation for sorcery. Indeed, the later evidence in the case showed that he had called her the Witch of Stapenhill when he met her in the wood, and it was that which had angered her.

His fits continued for three months. In April, Alse

Gooderidge was brought to the house to confront her alleged victim. Thomas at once had a fit, and scratched her face in an attempt to 'draw blood above the breath'. This ancient rite was not enough to break the spell, and the witch herself strenuously denied that she had ever practised magic upon the boy, or that she had any previous knowledge of him. She admitted meeting him on the day of the hare-hunt, but said she had mistaken him for another child who had once played her a mischievous trick, and it was because of this that she had spoken sharply to him. Two days later, she and her mother were arrested, and searched for witch-marks, which were found upon them both.

Alse Gooderidge was sent to Derby Prison, and while she was there, she confessed that she had in fact bewitched young Darling. She had, she said, a familiar spirit in the form of a red-and-white dog named Minny, which she had received from her mother. When the boy was rude to her in the wood, she had sent this familiar to torment him in every part of his body. The dog had followed him to his home in Burton, and that night his troubles began. She does not seem to have made any effort to take off the spell, and perhaps she was not able to do so. Before her trial she was taken to Burton Hall for a further examination, and was once more faced with Thomas, who immediately fell into thirty-seven fits in succession. She told the justices he would never mend unless they sought help, but they could have such help if they would. It is not clear whether she was referring to her own magic, or to exorcism; before she could explain further, she had a choking fit which prevented her from speaking for some minutes, and when she recovered, she said no more on the subject. Shortly afterwards she was brought to trial before Sir Edward Anderson. She was condemned to death, but she died in prison before the date fixed for her execution.

Darling's fits continued after her death, and his family called in John Darrell, a noted exorcist of the time. He was a very remarkable individual, whose career as an exorcist was partly responsible for the ecclesiastical rule embodied in the Canons of London which forbade clergymen of the Church of England to cast out devils without licence from their Bishop. At Cambridge he studied Law, but later on, he became a preacher, and was subsequently ordained. In 1586, he was asked to exorcise Katharine Wright, a seventeen-year-old girl who lived in

Mansfield, his native town. This he did, and she then accused a certain Margaret Roper of bewitching her. Darrell supported this accusation, but George Foljambe, the magistrate, who heard the case, discharged the accused woman, and reproved Darrell for his part in the affair, threatening him with imprisonment if he did anything of the kind again.

The young preacher must certainly have disregarded the magistrate's warning, for when we next hear of him ten years

*A servant of Nicholas Starkie taking her child to be 'dispossessed' by
Hartlay the conjurer*

later, he was already well known as an exorcist. Soon after he had dispossessed Thomas Darling he was called, with another minister, George More, to free the children and servants of Nicholas Starkie at Cleworth from the fiends which apparently tormented them. In 1594, Starkie's two children, John and Anne, began to suffer from fits and nervous shouting. A travelling conjuror named Edmund Hartlay was called in, and under his treatment, the children improved considerably in health. For eighteen months, he visited them at regular intervals, and so long as he did so, all was well. When, however, he declared his intention of leaving the district, John immediately became very ill, and vomited blood so freely that his life was thought to be in danger. Hartlay stopped the vomiting, and the grateful father then invited him to live permanently in his house. To this he agreed, but a dispute about his pay led to further trouble. Because he could not have what he wanted, he unwisely threatened his employer with still greater afflictions, and on the same day, the malady spread to three little girls who lived at Cleworth as Starkie's wards, and also to two women servants. All were afflicted with violent fits, vomiting of blood, involuntary crying and shouting, barking, and other hysterical symptoms. Hartlay remained to treat them, but his threats, and their apparent fulfilment were remembered against him later.

The house now became almost impossible to live in, and the conjuror, who had previously relied on charms and herbs, resorted to the more powerful, but illegal, device of the magic circle. He may have been spurred to this dangerous action by the fact that the demons attacked him as well as his patients. We are told that he also was 'tormented', which probably means that he was affected by the prevailing hysteria. On the day following this attack, he took his employer to a wood near Whalley, and there traced out a circle with four divisions and four crosses, and invited Starkie to tread it out, as he might not do so himself. What other rites were performed in this wood we do not know, but whatever they may have been, they were not successful in their object. No cure followed, and Starkie began to entertain doubts as to his healer's powers. He therefore sought for other help, and approached Dr Dee, who was then Warden of Manchester College. Dee refused to do anything, and advised him to seek the aid of godly preachers; he also sharply rebuked Hartlay. The conjuror seems to have taken offence at Starkie's action, and when, some time later, the children went to Manchester and called on Dr Dee, he told them it would be better for them not to desert an old friend for one new and untried. Three days later, all the afflicted persons became very much worse, and Hartlay himself had another hysterical fit, probably induced by rage.

This was the second time that a disagreement with the

conjuror had been followed by more violent symptoms in the patients, and suspicion now fell upon him. It was suggested that instead of helping the bewitched people, he was himself the cause of their trouble. One of the servants, Margaret Byrom, declared that the Devil had appeared to her in Hartlay's likeness on two nights in succession. When confronted by him, she fell to the ground and became quite speechless. The children also, when questioned, were unable to say anything except that Hartlay would not suffer them to speak against him. It must be said here that they never willingly said anything to his detriment, and seem to have been very fond of him throughout, though according to George More's account, on his last visit to the house, they all became very violent, and had to be forcibly prevented from striking him in their convulsions.

Hartlay was examined by Matthew Palmer, Dr Dee's curate, and was put to the test of repeating the Lord's Prayer. He broke down in this, and was unable to finish it. He was then taken before two justices of the peace, and was later sent to Lancaster for trial. The evidence against him was not conclusive until Starkie related the story of the magic circle. This proved to be his undoing, and he was condemned, and hanged as a witch in March 1597. How far he was really guilty of malicious witchcraft is very doubtful. His contemporaries always spoke of him as a conjuror, and it is probable that his true profession was that of a white witch and faith-healer. In Starkie's remarkable household he found ample scope for his gifts. The children and servants seem to have suffered from contagious hysteria, and he was undoubtedly able to influence them in their fits, and to hold their affection and trust. We have no reason to suppose that he did not honestly try to help them so far as his limited knowledge and rather unsteady character would permit. The threats used in his quarrels with the somewhat credulous master of Cleworth need not, perhaps, be taken very seriously; they were of an extremely vague character, and may not have had any real connection with witchcraft at all. He was plainly a hot-tempered and excitable man, and the general atmosphere at Cleworth was not such as to encourage discretion and restraint. It may well be that his chief fault was neither dishonesty nor malice, but simply an overbearing vanity which led him to undertake a task beyond his powers.

His death did not release the seven patients from their sufferings. Nicholas Starkie, having tried the older remedy of magic without success, now turned to exorcism, and invited Darrell and George More to his house. It is from the accounts written by these two men that we know most of the details of the Cleworth possession.[2] They arrived on 16 March, and at once began a strenuous course of prayer, fasting, and preaching. The operation took three days; at the end of that time, the demons fled, and six of the patients sprang from the floor on which they lay, and began to dance and shout out praises to God because they were cured. The seventh, Jane Ashton, was not freed until the next day, and later in her life, she once more fell into the power of the Devil, a circumstance sufficiently explained for the Puritan Darrell by the fact that she was a Roman Catholic. John Starkie lived to be one of the two magistrates who examined Edmund Robinson at Padiham in 1634, and it was perhaps because of his own unhappy experience as a child that he accepted that lying tale so readily.

The Cleworth case was the high mark of Darrell's career. Eight months afterwards, he undertook to dispossess an apprentice, one William Somers, of Nottingham, and apparently did so with success. Somers declared that he had been bewitched by Alice Freeman and twelve other women, all of whom were arrested, though only two were held for trial. Darrell asserted his belief in the boy's story, but certain circumstances had already aroused suspicion, and Somers was taken to the House of Correction to be questioned. Here he confessed that his supposed possession by the Devil was a mere fraud, and added that he had acted under Darrell's instructions. This was, of course, a very serious accusation to bring against a minister, and the Archbishop of York, to whom the matter was reported, set up a commission of enquiry. Somers was again questioned, but this time he retracted his confession, and fell into such violent fits before the commissioners that they were all convinced he was bewitched.

Alice Freeman was then brought to trial before Sir Edward Anderson who had already been concerned in the trial of Alse Gooderidge. He was not at all happy about this case, however, and urged Somers to state clearly whether his accusation was true or not. The boy admitted that it was not, whereupon the judge released the prisoner and wrote to the Archbishop of Canterbury. Darrell and More were summoned to Lambeth to be examined by the Archbishop, the Bishop of London, and others, including Samuel Harsnett, who afterwards wrote a book called *A Discovery of the fraudulent practises of John Darrel, Bachelor of Arts* (1599). Amongst the witnesses were Darling and Somers, both of whom confessed that their possession by the Devil and the subsequent exorcism were unreal and faked. Somers further added that he had been secretly taught by Darrell to pose as a possessed person, and to imitate the tricks performed by Katharine Wright in Mansfield thirteen years before. More hotly defended his friend. Neither minister would admit to fraud, either before or after their condemnation, and both wrote vigorous vindications of their conduct during their imprisonment. Both were deposed from the ministry, and imprisoned for a year in the Gatehouse. Many people continued to believe in them, but their careers as ministers and exorcists were ended. There can be little doubt that Darrell, at least, was justly convicted of imposture. Probably he began honestly enough, but the temptation to profit by the dishonesty of others, and to bolster up his reputation by doubtful methods, was in the end too much for him. After his release, he disappeared from public life, and we hear no more of him as an opponent of witchcraft. His more permanent memorial is the 72nd Canon of the Canons of London, drawn up by Bishop Bancroft in 1604, which forbids any clergyman of the Church of England to attempt, without the licence and sanction of his Bishop, 'upon any pretence whatever, either of possession or obsession, by fasting or prayer, to cast out any devil or devils, under pain of the imputation of imposture or cozenage, and deposition from the ministry'.

In 1675, Mary Moor, of Clayton, in Yorkshire, a girl of sixteen, was responsible, by slander, for the deaths of Joseph Hinchcliffe, and of Susan, his wife. She alleged that she had heard Susan and her daughter, Anne, plotting together to destroy the life of Martha Haigh, who lived in the district. She also stated that Joseph Hinchcliffe was concerned in this conspiracy as well. Hinchcliffe and his wife were bound over to answer the charge at the next Assizes, but in the meantime, there was a most unusual outburst of indignation against Mary

Moor amongst the local people. More than fifty individuals came forward and signed a petition in favour of the accused, stating that,

> Some of us have well known the said Susan and Anne, by the space of twenty years and upwards, others of us fifteen years and upwards; others of us ten years and upwards. And have by the said space observed and known the life and conversation of the said Susanna to be not only sober, orderly, and unblameable in every respect; but also of good example, and very helpful and useful in the neighbourhood, according to her poor ability. That she was a constant frequenter of public ordinances while she was able, and to the best of our understanding, made conscience of her ways in more than common sort. That we never heard, or had the least ground to suspect her and her said daughter, to be in any sort guilty of so foul a crime, but do fully believe that the said information against them both is a most gross and groundless (if not malicious) prosecution. And this we humbly certify as our very true apprehensions, as in the sight and presence of Him who will judge the secrets of all hearts. And as touching the said girl who now informs, some of us could say too much concerning her of a quite different nature, but that we judge recrimination to be an indirect way of clearing the innocent.[3]

Unfortunately, this heartfelt protest was not enough to help the unhappy Hinchcliffes. Before the next Assizes came round, Joseph Hinchcliffe, in despair, had hanged himself in a wood near his house. His corpse was not discovered until four days later, and in the meantime, his wife also had died, of grief and worry, praying on her deathbed for her accusers.

Jennet Preston

7 Witch-bands

Traditions of an organised, pagan witch-cult were never very plentiful in England, though they did exist occasionally, especially in the later years of the witch-belief. They were never really strong, and after the end of the persecution in the early eighteenth century, they disappeared altogether. There were, however, a few witch-trials in which the accused persons were shown to have banded together, and worked together in a given district, and in which their confessions, and the evidence of witnesses, does suggest the possible existence of an organised cult in that particular area.

One of the most celebrated witch-trials of the sixteenth century was that which took place at St Osyth, in Essex, in the year 1582. Thirteen alleged witches were involved, accused of having murdered, between them, some twenty-four persons, besides injuring others who did not die, and harming cattle and other livestock. One of those accused was Ursley Kempe (or Grey), a woman of doubtful reputation, and locally suspected of witchcraft, who practised as a midwife. She had a bastard son named Thomas Rabbet, then eight years old, and this child testified against his mother before Brian Darcy, one of the examining justices. He said she possessed four familiar spirits, all in the form of small animals. One was a grey cat named Tyttey, and another was a black cat called Jack. A third was a toad, whose name was Pygine, and the fourth was a white lamb called Tyffin. This last was distinctly curious, since it was generally believed that no witch's familiar could take the form of a dove or a lamb because both these were sacred symbols. Young Thomas asserted he had seen his mother feeding these creatures on white bread, or cake, and giving them beer to drink. He added that during the night they came to her and sucked blood from her arms and other parts of her body.

During her own examination, Ursley confirmed her son's story, and admitted that she had sent Jack, the black cat, to torment her sister-in-law, and eventually to cause her death, 'for that her sister had called her whore and witch'. She also confessed that, having fallen out with a neighbour named Grace Thurlowe, she had killed the latter's baby by sending Tyffin, the white lamb, to rock its cradle until it fell over, and the child, being thrown out of it on to the floor, broke its neck. All these, and other crimes, she confessed with tears; but she also implicated others in her confessions, and eventually thirteen or fourteen women were accused of crimes ranging from murder to barn-burning.

Most of these were acquitted or, if found guilty, were reprieved, but Ursley Kempe and Elisabeth Bennet were hanged. Ursley Kempe had informed against Elisabeth in the first instance, saying that she kept at least one familiar spirit, and that she, Ursley, knew this to be a fact because she herself had seen it. Going one day to Elisabeth's house and finding everybody out, she had peered through the window and had seen 'a spirit lift up a cloth, lying over a pot, looking much like a Ferret'. As a result of this statement, Elisabeth Bennet was brought before the justices, and admitted that she did possess familiars, not one, but two. It seemed, however, that neither of these spirits resembled a ferret, 'one called Suckin being black like a Dog, the other called Lierd being red like a Lion'.[1] She further confessed that, with the aid of Suckin, she had murdered William Byett, a farmer, and his wife, because the man had insulted her, 'calling her old trot, old whore, and other lewd speeches', and had refused to let her have milk when she needed it. For these murders she was hanged; and so also was Ursley Kempe, for the murder of her sister-in-law and Grace Thurlowe's baby, and a number of other witchcraft crimes of which she was convicted.

A very sad story of suspicion and terror was told by one of the witnesses of this case. Richard Harrison, parson of Beamond, stated that he and his late wife had lived at Little Okeley, in a house belonging to her, and there, 'about Summer was twelvemonth', she had a duck sitting on some eggs under a cherry-tree in the hedge. When the eggs were hatched, the ducklings were missing, and his wife at once suspected Annis Herd, a local woman of bad reputation, of having stolen them. She therefore went at once to the woman's house, and there 'rated her and all too chid her', but, as her husband recorded, 'could get no knowledge of her ducklings, and so came home and was very angry against the said Annis'.

She was not only angry, she was afraid. Richard Harrison's testimony continued:

... within a short time after, the said Richard Harrison went into a chamber, and there did read on his books for the space of 2 or 3 hours, bidding his said wife to go to bed with the children, and that he would come to her, and so she did: and being awhile laid down in her bed, his wife did cry out: Oh Lord, Lord, help me and keep me, and he running to her, asked her what she ailed? and she said, Oh Lord, I am sore afraid, and have been divers times, but that I would not tell you, and said, I am in doubt, husband, that yonder wicked harlot, Annis Herd, doth bewitch me, and ye said Richard Harrison said to his wife, I pray you be content and think not so, but trust in God and put your trust in him only, and he will defend you from her, and from the Devil himself also: and said moreover, what will the people say, that I being a Preacher should have my wife so weak in faith.

This examinate saith that within two months after, his said

wife said unto him, I pray you as ever there was love between us (as I hope there hath been for I have v pretty children by you I thank God) seek some remedy for me against yonder wicked beast (meaning the said Annis Herd). And if you will not, I will complain to my father, and I think he will see some remedy for me, for (said she), if I have no remedy, she will utterly consume me, whereupon this examinate did exhort his wife as he had before, and desired her to pray to God, and that he would hang her the said Annis Herd if he could prove any such matter. . . .

A little later, when he was in the parsonage garden gathering plums, Annis Herd came to the hedge side and asked him to give her some fruit. He answered angrily, 'I am glad you are here, you vile strumpet . . . I do think you have bewitched my wife, and as truly as God doth live, if I can perceive that she be troubled any more as she hath been, I will not leave a whole bone about thee, and besides I will seek to have thee hanged . . .'. He went on to threaten her with the anger of his father-in-law, and to reproach her with having bewitched the livestock of various people in the village. Finally, 'as he was coming down of the tree, she, the said Annis, did suddenly depart from him without having any plums'.

But she had her revenge, or so at least, he believed. He stated in evidence that

before Christmas, his said wife was taken sore sick & was at many times afraid both sleeping and waking, & did call this examinate her husband unto her not two days before her death, and said unto him, husband, God bless you and your children, and God send you good friends, for I must depart from you, for I am now utterly consumed with yonder wicked Creature, naming the said Annis Herd, which words, he saith, were spoken by her in the presence of John Pollin & mother Poppe, and within two days after this his said wife departed out of this world in a perfect faith, repeating these words, Oh Annis Herd, Annis Herd, she hath consumed me.[2]

In spite of this accusation, and the testimony of other witnesses that Annis Herd had bewitched their cattle and pigs, their milk and their ale, she was acquitted.

Although so many women in St Osyth were apparently practising witches, there is no real evidence that they were members of a religious cult, or even of a secular company formed for mutual help, or protection. No mention of any such secret organisation was made by their accusers, or by witnesses, and certainly, it would have been recorded if the existence of such an organisation had been suspected. In so small a place, the witches must obviously have known each other, and probably most of their secret activities were known as well. Ursley Kempe knew enough about Elisabeth Bennet and Alice Hunt to inform against them both, but she did not suggest that she and they had ever worked together in any magical enterprise. Apart from her window-peering, she said that she gained her knowledge of her neighbours' actions from her own familiar, Tyffin, who 'did tell her always (when she asked) what the other witches had done'.

Thirty years later, in 1612, the celebrated trials of the Lancaster witches brought to light what appears to have been a genuine company of witches in Pendle Forest. Originally, this had consisted of the members of two Forest families and some of their friends and neighbours, but about 1601 a quarrel between the leaders of both households had split the ranks. Thereafter, there were two companies operating in the region, each at enmity with the other, and doing its best to harm, not only the members but also the supporters, of the opposing party.

In 1612, both sets of witches fell into trouble, and nineteen among them were brought to trial in Lancaster. From the evidence and confessions at these trials, carefully recorded by Thomas Potts, then clerk of the court,[3] it appeared that, as far back as 1591, Elisabeth Southerns, a woman locally known as Old Demdike, encountered what she described as 'a Spirit or Devil in the shape of a Boy' near a stone-pit in the Forest. This spirit, who said his name was Tibb, demanded her soul, and promised to give her whatever she might ask in exchange. To this she agreed and, for the next five or six years, he appeared to her at intervals, sometimes as a man, sometimes in the form of a brown dog or a black cat, to enquire what she needed. Having thus become a witch herself, she proceeded to initiate her son, Christopher Howgate, her daughter, Elisabeth Device, and the latter's children, James and Alison. She also persuaded

Anne Whittle (alias Chattox) to give her soul to another spirit who, in the form of 'a thing like a Christian man' had been importuning her to do so for some time. Anne consented at last, and the spirit said, 'Thou shalt want nothing; and be revenged of whom thou list'. Thereafter she and Elisabeth, along with their children and grandchildren and some of their neighbours, banded together to practise witchcraft in the Forest, and for a number of years established a sort of reign of terror over the innocent inhabitants of the region.

The lasting feud between the two families began about eleven years before the trials, when the fire-house belonging to the Devices was broken into, and a quantity of linen clothes, and also meal, was stolen from it. On the Sunday following the theft, Alison Device saw Ann Redfearn, Old Chattox's married daughter, wearing a band and a coif, which she declared to be part of the stolen goods. The subsequent quarrel spread to the two older witches, who rushed to the defence of their daughters, and from having long been friends and allies, they became bitter enemies. Alison's father, John Device, was, however, so afraid of Anne Chattox's revenge that he agreed to pay her blackmail, in the form of a yearly dole of meal, if she would agree not to harm him or his. He actually did so until he died some time later. This seems to suggest that he considered her a more powerful witch than his mother-in-law, Elisabeth Southerns, or his wife, either of whom should have been able to protect him by her own magic. But the most serious effect of the rift between the households was not to be averted by any blackmail payment. The rival factions knew too much about each other's activities, past and present, and when both families, and their supporters, fell into the hands of the Law, they gave vent to their malice by freely accusing their one-time accomplices of crimes committed both before and after the quarrel.

Towards the end of March 1612, Roger Nowell, one of the local Justices of the Peace, was stirred by the steadily increasing number of complaints against them, to examine four of the Forest witches – Elisabeth Southerns, Anne Whittle, Alison Device, and Anne Redfearn. They all admitted their own witchcraft and implicated some others, and they were committed to Lancaster Castle until they could be tried at the next Assizes. On the Good Friday following these events, a meeting was

Old Chattox

called at Malkin Tower, the home of Old Demdike. According to James Device, who was present, the principal business of this meeting was, firstly, to name Alison Device's familiar spirit (which they did not do because she was not there), and, secondly, to devise some means of delivering the witches then in prison. This they hoped to achieve by murdering the gaoler, and blowing up the building before the next Assizes. Besides this, they discussed methods of helping Jennet Preston, of Gisborne-in-Craven, who had come to ask their aid because she wished to kill Thomas Lister, of Westby, and found her own magical powers not strong enough to do so without assistance. At the end of the meeting, when they were leaving, they agreed to meet again in twelve months' time at Jennet Preston's house, and she promised to make them a great feast on that occasion. It was mercifully hidden from them that long before the twelve months were past, most of those present, as well as the witches already in the Castle, would be dead.

Because the gathering at Malkin Tower began with a feast of stolen mutton, it has often been spoken of as one of the very few known English examples of a Witches' Sabbat. In fact, the evidence for this is very slight. It is true that a noonday meal was eaten by all present. James Device confessed at his trial that on the night before the meeting he stole a wether belonging to John Robinson, of Barley, and brought it to his grandmother's house, where it was killed, and eaten on the following day. Nothing seems to distinguish this repast from an ordinary meal shared by friends in a time of anxiety, nor do the subsequent proceedings suggest anything of a religious or magical nature. No devil presided over the feast, or the discussions. There were no sacrifices, no adoration of Satan, no bringing-in of new converts, no dancing or singing or carousing. Undoubtedly, there was an urgent meeting of witches accustomed to work together, alarmed now by the action of the authorities, and anxious to save their imprisoned friends before it was too late; but of anything of a more mystical or ritual character, there seems to be little or no proof.

By the end of April, Elisabeth and James Device were arrested, and one by one, the other Forest witches were taken until some eighteen persons were in custody awaiting trial. Some others escaped by flight; Elisabeth Southerns died in prison before the Assizes began, and so never came to trial. Her granddaughter, Alison Device, who was young and had not long been a witch, confessed to owning a familiar spirit in the shape of a black dog. This spirit was not yet named, as we have seen, but she had already used it to lame a pedlar named John Law, who had refused to let her have some pins. At her trial, she freely admitted having done so, and when confronted with the crippled pedlar (who seems to have had some sort of stroke), she wept most bitterly. But a few weeks earlier, in her examination by Roger Nowell, she had readily accused her grandmother of having bewitched Richard Baldwin's child, so that it died, and also of destroying by witchcraft John Nutter's sick cow, when she had been called in to heal it.

All the prisoners testified very freely against each other, as well as acknowledging their own offences, with the exception of the doubtfully guilty Alice Nutter,* who kept her own counsel till the end. Elisabeth Device's child, Jennet, too young to be an active witch herself, brought a good deal of evidence against her mother, her brother, and some other witches who had been at the Malkin Tower meeting. Her appearance in court as a witness was scarcely legal, since the Law required witnesses to be at least fourteen years old, and she was only nine, but this was not the only case in which this requirement was disregarded. She was so small that she had to stand upon a table in the middle of the court-room, so that all present could see her, and there she calmly swore away the lives of her nearest relatives. When Elisabeth Device saw her, she broke into such frenzied ravings and cursings that she had to be removed before the child could speak. Once order had been restored, however, she spoke to some purpose; she seems to have been a very observant child, blessed with a good memory, and totally devoid of any family loyalty.

Jennet Preston, who had so confidently invited all those at the Good Friday meeting to feast with her twelve months hence, was the first of the company to perish. During the summer, Thomas Lister had died, and in his last moments, he had cried out against her. When he was dead, she was made to touch the corpse, and at once it bled. It was universally believed then, and

*Executed in August 1612. See page 84.

much later, that a murdered person's corpse would bleed at the touch of, or even in the presence of, his murderer. The recorder of her trial remarked that such bleeding 'hath ever been held a great argument to induce a Jury to hold him guilty that shall be accused of Murder, and hath seldom, or never, failed in the Trial'. It had a strong effect in this case. Jennet Preston was tried at York on 27 July. Unlike her Lancashire colleagues, she confessed nothing, but the evidence given by some of the other witches as to her presence at the Malkin Tower meeting, and the bleeding of the corpse convinced the jury that she was guilty of murder by witchcraft. She was accordingly condemned, and in due course, she was executed.

When the York Assizes were ended, the Judges moved to Lancaster, and the trial of the prisoners in the Castle began. Most of them were accused of murder, or of causing grievous bodily harm, as Alison Device did in the case of John Law. Some sixteen deaths in the neighbourhood were ascribed to their malicious powers, as well as damage done to cattle and other forms of property. Several admitted to the possession of familiars. James Device had one in the shape of a black dog called Dancy, by whose help and advice he was able to kill Mistress Towneley, of the Carre. He also told a rather sinister story implicating both his grandmother and himself. Two years before he said, 'on Sheare Thursday',* Old Demdike bade him go to church and receive Communion, but not to eat the Bread. Instead, he was to bring it away with him, and give it 'to such a thing as should meet him on his way homewards'. In spite of these instructions, he did swallow the bread. Coming back from the church, he encountered a hare, who asked him whether he had brought the bread, as his grandmother had told him to do. He said he had not, whereupon the hare fell into a rage, and threatened to tear him to pieces. James hastily crossed himself, and at once the demon-hare vanished, and was seen no more.

At the end of the trials, ten prisoners stood condemned to die – Anne Whittle (or Chattox), Elisabeth, James and Alison Device, Anne Redfearn, Alice Nutter, John and Jane Bulcock, Isabel Robey, and Katharine Hewet. Old Demdike and Jennet Preston were already dead. Margaret Pearson, who had only

*Maundy Thursday.

killed a horse, was sentenced to a year's imprisonment, and four
appearances in the pillory, upon Market Day, in the four towns
of Clitheroe, Padiham, Whalley, and Lancaster. The rest were
acquitted. We hear no more of those who fled when Roger
Nowell first began his enquiries. No doubt they returned to
their homes when the excitement had died down, and continued
to practise magic in secret. Probably, also, they handed on their
knowledge to the next generation. In so remote and uncultivated
a district, it is unlikely that the old tradition would have been
allowed to die out because of one serious set-back; and certainly,
when Edmund Robinson startled the magistrates in 1634 with
his improbable story, he was able to mention the names of
several local people who had been suspected of witchcraft before
ever he accused them.

In 1673, a girl named Anne Armstrong told a very peculiar
tale to the Morpeth justices concerning a witchcraft organisation
supposed to exist in Northumberland. She was a maidservant
employed by Mrs Mabel Fouler, of Burtree House, near
Stocksfield-on-Tyne. One day, her mistress sent her to buy eggs
from Anne Forster, of Stocksfield, but she did not succeed in
doing so because the two women could not agree about the
price. In the course of the discussion, Anne asked the egg-
vendor to sit down 'and look her head', that is, to search her
head for lice. This was a service that simple people often
rendered to each other at that time, and Mrs Forster was neither
surprised nor offended. She did as she was asked, and then the
girl did the same for her. She went home afterwards, and
thought no more about it, but three days later, when she was
fetching the cows from the pasture at daybreak, she met an old
man in ragged clothes, who warned her that Mrs Forster was a
witch, and would be the first to ride Anne's spirit like a horse,
but that other witches would do the same. They would try to
allure her, he said, by many tricks, but if she did not eat any of
their food, she would be safe. Finally, he spoke of a piece of
cheese which she would find lying beside her one day when she
had fallen asleep in a field, with her apron over her head, and
which she would eat. Having said all this, he departed, and Anne
fell down in a swoon which lasted for several hours, after which
she arose and went home, 'but kept all these things secret'.

This long swoon seems to have been the first of many, for

according to her own story, she was subject from then on to similar fits almost every day, and often by night as well. She found the cheese and ate it, as had been predicted, and thereafter she appears to have fallen into the power of the local witches. One night, just before Christmas, and soon after she had recovered from one of her faints, she saw Anne Forster coming towards her with a bridle in her hand, which bridle she threw over the girl's head, and forthwith rode her, like a horse, to Riding Mill Bridge, where the witches frequently met. On arrival there, the bridle was taken off, and Anne at once assumed her human shape again. She saw thirteen persons gathered there, three of whom she already knew, and subsequently named in her statements to the justices. She also saw their Leader, whom she described as 'a long black man riding on a bay galloway, as she thought, which they called their protector'. She was told to sing to the company, and did so, while they danced on the bridge-end in various animal-shapes, such as hares, cats, mice, and several other forms. At the end of the evening, they all rode home again, with their 'protector' leading the way, and Mrs Forster riding upon her bridled victim, now once more a horse, as before.

Anne mentioned several other meetings, to which the witches forced her to go by threats of worse things to come. At one, held at John Newton's house on 3 April, she saw 'five coveys consisting of thirteen persons in every covey'. At this gathering there was a great feast, over which the 'protector whom they called their god' presided, sitting in a golden chair. A rope hung down from the ceiling, and every witch pulled on it, and so obtained whatever he or she wanted to eat, in the manner described forty years before by Edmund Robinson in Lancashire. We hear of boiled capons, beef and mutton, plum broth, wine and ale (but no water), as well as butter and cheese, and wheat-flour wherewith to make pies. On another occasion, when she was ridden by Jane Baites, of Corbridge, to a place the name of which she could not remember, she saw that the presiding devil had placed a stone in the centre of the ring of witches. She did not relate what kind of stone it was, but she said that all the witches 'set themselves down, and bending towards the stone, repeated the Lord's Prayer backwards . . .'.

It is difficult to know what to make of this extraordinary

story. Anne Armstrong does not seem to have been a reliable witness, and in posing as a purely unwilling participant in the witch-rites, she was almost certainly lying. Exactly what she was trying to convey by her wild tales is not clear. The incident of the stone before which the witches bowed down and recited the Lord's Prayer in a twisted and blasphemous manner, and the frequent references to their Leader as 'their god' or 'their blessed saviour' suggest a cult-organisation, thinly but fairly widely spread over that part of Northumberland. The covens that she mentions do often consist of thirteen persons which, according to Dr Margaret Murray, was 'the fixed number among the witches of Great Britain',[4] but their gatherings as Anne described them bear little resemblance to the Sabbats of tradition. The dances performed by the witches were apparently ritual dances, and involved a ritual animal-disguise, usually as cats, or hares, or the like, but sometimes as bees or birds. The power of transformation was evidently highly prized by the individual witches, as for instance, in the case of Ann Baites, of Morpeth, who turned herself successively into a cat, a hare, a greyhound, and a bee, in order to let the Devil see how many different shapes she could assume.

The same power was sometimes used in bewitching ordinary people and their cattle. Mary Hunter and Dorothy Green told the Devil in Anne's hearing that they had enchanted John March's mare so that it died. He himself stated in evidence at Morpeth Sessions that one evening, about sunset, he was riding home when a swallow suddenly appeared, and began weaving and fluttering about his mare, under and over her and round-about. He struck at it repeatedly with his whip, but he could not drive it away until at last it went of its own accord. The mare was then quite well, but within four days of her return home, she became first frantic, and then blind, and on the fourth day, she died.

There were also instances of more ordinary witchcraft. Other horses and cattle were bewitched in a variety of different ways, and sicknesses and other misfortunes were inflicted upon various people. Anne said in evidence that she knew this was so because she had heard the witches concerned confess their crimes to the Devil. One woman, Elisabeth Pickering, of Wittingstall, confessed that she had killed a neighbour's child by magic, or rather, she boasted of it, because the Devil rewarded those who did the most harm to their neighbours. But in general it is noteworthy that the evil that these witches were supposed to have done was far less serious than that committed in Pendle Forest, or at St Osyth, and even their ritual offences seem to have been somewhat erratic and selective. It seems likely that a certain amount of witchcraft was practised in this district, as elsewhere, and that Anne was mixed up in this; but that all the rest, or most of it, was the result of her embroideries. All the accused witches denied their guilt, and the result of the trials is not now certain. The people named were all examined, and two were kept in prison for a short time, but there is no record of any other punishment, and probably they were all acquitted.[5]

The most detailed account of an English witch-organisation is that preserved in the confessions of the Somerset witches who were tried in 1664. Two full covens – one at Wincanton and the other at Brewham – were presided over by the same Chief, or Devil, who was known to his followers as 'the Man in black' because he normally appeared in the form of a rather small man, dressed in black clothes, and wearing a little band. On joining one or other of the two covens, the witches signed a contract with the Man in black, apparently for a term of years. Elisabeth Style said that he promised her money, and that she 'should live gallantly, and have the pleasure of the World for Twelve years if she would with her Blood sign his Paper, which was to give her Soul to him'. When the witches came to the place appointed for one of their meetings, they called out 'Robin!', and their Chief then appeared. Elisabeth Style and Alice Hunt also called on him by name when they needed something, and particularly, if they desired to work some evil. He then appeared to them, sometimes as a man and sometimes as a black dog, or in some other form. Before Elisabeth Style made her request, she used to say 'O Sathan, give me thy purpose'.

He fixed the date and place of the meetings, which were usually held at night. The witches flew to and from these gatherings, by means of a greenish oil and certain magical words. At the start of the proceedings, when the Man in black first appeared, all made obeisance to him, 'and the little Man put his hand to his Hat, saying How do ye? speaking *low* but *big*'.[6] The lowness of his voice is mentioned elsewhere in these confessions also, and this perhaps suggests that he wore a mask which deadened the sound. When the company sat down to their meal, he presided over it, having first supplied all the food, which was served upon a white tablecloth. 'They had', said Elisabeth Style, 'Wine, Cakes, and Roast Meat (all brought by the Man in black) which they did eat and drink. They danced and were merry, and were bodily there, and in their Cloathes.'[7]

In the serious part of the meetings, the witches frequently brought 'pictures', or waxen images, of their enemies, and presented them to their Chief who baptised them, and named them for those in whose likeness they were made. Ann Bishop (the Officer of the Wincanton coven) brought an image made of blackish wax, which the Man in black baptised by the name of John Newman, after which he, and Ann herself, both thrust thorns into it. On another occasion, Margaret Agar presented an image for baptism, and after this ceremony had been performed, the Man in black stuck a thorn into the crown of its head. Then Margaret Agar stabbed it in the breast with another thorn, and Catherine Green did the same in the side, after which its maker threw it on the ground saying, 'There is Cornish's Picture with a Murrain on it.' Several other people are named in the confessions as having been similarly bewitched during the various meetings.

The investigations into this curious case were carried out with great energy and enthusiasm by Robert Hunt, one of the Somerset justices. They might have produced still more information than they did, but for the fact that his activities were checked, or at least discouraged, by the authorities. Joseph Glanvil, to whom he handed the records of the prisoners' confessions, wrote indignantly: 'Had not his discoveries and endeavours met with great opposition and discouragement by some then in Authority, the whole Clan of those hellish Confederates in these parts had been justly exposed and punished.'[8] All the same, he managed to bring a good deal to light, including, perhaps, the rather mild nature of the English Sabbat, when compared with its Continental equivalent. It is said that some of the witches acknowledged that the Man in black was really the Devil, and perhaps they did, but actually, they do not really seem to have known who he was. He appeared at the beginning of a meeting, and disappeared at its end, and his true identity was never known. At the time of the trial, he disappeared as completely as he did at the end of the meetings, and so far as we know, was never seen or heard of again.

Margery Jourdemayne

8 Witchcraft in High Places

In the long history of witchcraft in England, as in other countries, the great majority of recorded cases necessarily concern more or less simple people, seeking comparatively simple ends by means of magic, and affecting comparatively few individuals by their sorcery. This is obviously natural, since there have always been more simple folk than those of any other sort. Nevertheless, all men, high or low, aristocratic or humble, are liable to much the same fears and hopes and desires as one another, and in the days when every one believed in the efficacy of magic, any one might turn to it for help. Undoubtedly, many men and women of high rank did so turn to it, and often they were accused of doing so when they were, in fact, innocent. Such aristocratic magicians were usually thought to be more dangerous than their humbler colleagues whose enchantments operated only in a narrow circle. A man whose position was

112

already assured had no need of spells to accomplish petty robberies or minor acts of malice, but his wider ambitions and opportunities might tempt him to influence the course of politics, or overthrow prelates and ministers who stood in his way, or shorten the lives of kings. His very position exposed him to accusations dictated by envy, hatred, and the simple destructive instinct to pull down that which is high.

Nor can it be seriously suggested that all such charges brought against the great were entirely without foundation, at least as far as intention and personal belief were concerned. When Adam de Stratton, Chancellor of the Exchequer, was arrested in 1289, he was charged with extortion and dishonesty, and was found to be in possession of an immense treasure, to which he had no right at all. There was also found in his keeping something quite unexpected. This was a silk bag containing some very curious objects, including strands of human hair, nail-parings, and the paws of toads and moles. These things instantly suggested sorcery to the startled discoverers, but de Stratton offered no explanation of them. He did, however, contrive to break the seal set upon the bag by the King's officers, and to throw away the incriminating contents before they could be used in evidence against him.[1]

In 1324, Dame Alice Kyteler, of Kilkenny in Ireland, was suddenly accused of witchcraft by her husband, and charged before Richard de Ledrede, Bishop of Ossory. She was a wealthy woman, a member of an Anglo-Norman family long established in Kilkenny and, at the time of the trial, she had already been married four times. Her first three husbands had all left the bulk of their property to her, or to her son by her first marriage, William Outlawe, thereby impoverishing the rest of her children. In 1324, her fourth husband, Sir John le Poer, was suffering from a wasting disease which had already reduced him to a state of extreme emaciation, and seemed likely to bring about his death before very long. He does not appear to have suspected her, or any one else, of bewitching him until a maidservant in his household warned him that his wife might be responsible for his ailment. Then he demanded that she should give him her keys, and when she refused to do so, he took them by force. He found in her coffers certain objects strongly suggestive of sorcery, including magical powders and unguents.

Holinshed, in his *Chronicle of Ireland* (1587) says that among these things was a sacramental wafer stamped with the devil's name, and also some ointment 'wherewith she greased a staff, upon which she ambled and gallopped through thick and thin, when and in what manner she listed'. Contemporary records of the case do not, however, mention these two items, and it may be that they are later additions to the tale; but with or without them, Sir John found more than enough to alarm him. Without further delay, he sent all the evidence directly to the Bishop of Ossory by the hands of two friars.

The Bishop had already heard rumours of witchcraft in his diocese, and he now ordered a very stringent enquiry into the case of Dame Alice. As a result of the inquisition, she was accused, not only of murdering her first three husbands and of enchanting Sir John, but also of denying Christ and His Church, and of leading a number of local people along the paths of heresy and devil-worship. She and her followers, it was alleged, sacrificed living creatures to demons at the cross-roads, tearing them to pieces, and using their entrails, along with other horrible things, in the preparation of ointments and powders for use in evil magic. She also consorted carnally with a familiar spirit named Robin Artisson, who was curiously described as *ex pauperioribus inferni,* one of the proletariat of Hell. This spirit appeared to her in various forms, sometimes as a cat, or as a shaggy black dog, and sometimes as a black man of low stature. From him, she was said to have acquired her wealth, which probably means that he taught her how to bewitch the husbands who actually left it to her. Holinshed also mentions a spell she was supposed to have used for the benefit of her son. She was seen, he says, sweeping the streets of Kilkenny, 'between compline and twilight', raking all the dirt and rubbish from in front of the houses towards William Outlawe's house, and murmuring as she did so,

> To the house of William, my son,
> Hie all the wealth of Kilkenny town.[2]

A long-drawn and bitter battle between the Bishop and Dame Alice and her supporters followed the drawing-up of this lengthy indictment, which was complicated by legal and political considerations, and almost certainly by the fact that Richard de

Ledrede was an Englishman, and not very popular in his Irish diocese. Dame Alice was eventually cited to appear at Kilkenny and answer the charges made against her, but she escaped and fled to England. She was tried in her absence and condemned as a witch and a heretic but nothing more is certainly known about her. She is usually supposed to have lived quite peacefully in England for the rest of her life.

Of those accused with her, one escaped with her, but all the rest suffered punishment in one form or another. In most cases, the penalties seem to have been comparatively mild, but official records are lacking, and only the fate of Petronilla de Midia (or Meath) is certain. She confessed to taking part in all the crimes of which Dame Alice was accused, including the denial of Christianity, offering of sacrifices to Robin Artisson, and consulting with demons. She declared that Dame Alice was a far greater witch than she, and that throughout their association, she had been led and instructed by her. Perhaps because she had been a close friend of her leader as well as a follower, she was pursued with singular venom by the Bishop, who caused her to be flogged six times, and finally had her burnt. She was the first person to die thus for witchcraft in Ireland.

In 1419, Henry V accused his stepmother, Joan of Navarre, of attempting to murder him by magic. Exactly how she meant to do this is uncertain, but it was alleged in Parliament that she 'had compassed and imagined the death and destruction of our lord the king in the most horrible manner that one could devise'. Her confessor, a friar named John Randolf, acknowledged that he had taken part with her in 'sorcery and necromancy', and it was his statement which seems to have been the main support of the King's case. Yet the sentences pronounced upon both the Queen and the friar were strangely light, so light as to suggest that there may have been doubts in the King's mind. Queen Joan was committed to Leeds Castle in Sir John Pelham's charge, and her property was taken from her; but a few weeks before he died in 1422, Henry directed that her dower should be restored to her. As for John Randolf, he must surely have expected a death sentence, but he was merely imprisoned during the King's pleasure. In 1429, he was murdered by a mad priest who attacked him first with a stone and then with a hatchet, and hid the corpse under a dunghill.[3]

The romantic story of Elisabeth Woodville's meeting with Edward IV in Whittlebury Forest, under a tree long afterwards known as the Queen's Oak, and of his later secret marriage to her, seemed so amazing to many of his subjects that witchcraft appeared to them to be the only possible explanation. She was the daughter of Sir Richard Woodville, afterwards Baron Rivers, and his wife, Jacquetta, the widowed Duchess of Bedford. She was first married to Sir John Grey, who fought on the Lancastrian side at the second Battle of St Albans in 1461, and was killed there. When the Yorkists triumphed, her husband's estates were forfeited, and it was to plead for their restoration to her children that she is said to have waylaid Edward in Whittlebury Forest. Thus neither by rank nor by her family's political record, was she a really suitable wife for the King, and when at a Council meeting at Reading in 1464, he suddenly announced his intention of marrying her, his astonished Councillors hastened to point out that

> . . . she was not his match, however good and however fair she might be, and that he must know well that she was no wife for such a high prince as himself; for she was not the daughter of a duke or earl, but her mother the Duchess of Bedford had married a simple knight, so that though she was the child of a duchess and the niece of the Count of St Pol, still she was no wife for him.[4]

To these protests, and to the Councillors' advice to seek a wife elsewhere, Edward's reply was short and to the point. He said he would have no other wife but Elisabeth, and that 'such was his good pleasure'.

He had excellent reasons for refusing their advice, for he was married already. Fabyan relates in his *Chronicle* how

> . . . in the most secret manner, upon the first day of May, King Edward espoused Elisabeth, late the wife of Sir John Grey. . . . Which spousailles were solemnised early in the morning at the town of Grafton, near unto Stoney-Stratford. At which marriage was no person present but the *spouse*, the *spousesse*, the duchess of Bedford, her mother, the priest, and two gentlemen and a young man who helped the priest to sing.

The thing was done and had to be accepted. Three weeks after the Council meeting in Reading, Elisabeth was brought to Court and publicly acknowledged by the King as his wife, and by all present as their Queen.

A notion that the secret marriage had been contrived by sorcery on the part of the Duchess of Bedford seems to have existed in some circles from the beginning, and in later years it was strengthened by the unpopularity of Elisabeth's family. During a rising in 1469, when Edward was temporarily a captive in the hands of the Earl of Warwick, one, Thomas Wake, attempted to invalidate the marriage by accusing the Duchess of Bedford of securing the King's love for her daughter by means of image-magic. He brought forth a leaden image of a man-at-arms, about the length of a man's finger, broken in the middle, and 'made fast with a Wyre'. This he declared she had fashioned. He also called upon John Daunger, a parish clerk of Stoke Brewerne, in Northamptonshire, to bear witness that she had made two others, one representing Edward and the other Elisabeth. Unfortunately for Wake, the case was not heard until January 1470, by which time Edward was free again, and times had changed. John Daunger, his principal witness, refused to give the desired evidence, and asserted that he 'heard never no witchcraft of my lady of Bedford'. The Duchess was consequently cleared of the slanderous charges brought against her by Thomas Wake.[5]

It was not, however, the last that she and her daughter were to hear of the matter of sorcery. In April 1483, Edward died, and in the following month his brother, Richard of Gloucester, became Protector of the Realm, and of the young King, Edward V. Edward IV seems to have been singularly unfortunate in his brothers. George, Duke of Clarence, betrayed him more than once while he lived, and Richard's chief concern after his death was to usurp the throne. To achieve this end, he revived the old witchcraft-scandal in an attempt to prove that the Queen's marriage had never been valid, and that consequently, her son, Edward, was not now the true king. He also attacked Elisabeth herself as a witch, along with the late King's mistress, Jane Shore, whom he described as the Queen's accomplice.

In his *Historie of Kyng Richarde the Thirde,* Sir Thomas More described how, at a Council meeting in the Tower of London, held on 16 June, Richard suddenly demanded of the assembled

company what ought to be the punishment of those who conspired against his life. Having received the only possible answer,
he accused the Queen and Jane of wasting his body by magic,
and in proof of this thrust forth his withered arm before the
horrified Councillors, every one of whom was well aware,
according to More, that it had been withered since his birth. But
no one dared to say so. Lord Hastings hesitantly said that if the
two women had indeed done this, they deserved heinous
punishment, and was furiously reviled by Richard, arrested, and
executed that same afternoon on a pretext of involvement in an
alleged plot. Jane Shore was imprisoned in the Tower, her
property was confiscated, and she was subsequently made to do
public penance in the streets of London. Elisabeth could not be
touched, for she was in sanctuary at Westminster, whither she
had fled with her youngest son, the little Duke of York, as soon
as Richard seized power. On 26 June, the Duke of Gloucester
assumed the Crown, having declared his two royal nephews to
be bastards because of the nature of their parents' marriage. He
managed to obtain control of their persons and put them in the
Tower of London – and what happened to them thereafter is
still one of the mysteries of history.

A very famous witchcraft-trial in the fifteenth century was
that of Eleanor Cobham, Duchess of Gloucester, who was
charged in 1441 with conspiring with certain other people to
bring about the death of Henry VI by magic. She was the wife
of Humphrey, Duke of Gloucester, who was the King's uncle,
and Regent during his minority, and she was therefore already
near enough to the throne to make any magical practices of
which she might be suspected extremely dangerous. She was
accused of making enquiries into her own political future, and
also of causing a waxen image to be made which was intended,
according to the evidence, to destroy the King. She did not, of
course, make these enquiries herself because she had not the
requisite skill, nor could she construct the wax figure that was
to kill her nephew. She needed accomplices in the matter, and
these she had in the persons of two priests named Roger
Bolingbroke and Thomas Southwell, and that of a woman called
Margery Jourdemayne, who lived in the Manor of Eye-next-
Westminster, and was known as the Witch of Eye.

This woman seems to have been a straightforward witch who

might never have fallen into serious trouble had she not, unfortunately for herself, become involved in the affairs of a great lady. Before Eleanor Cobham was married, she is said to have gone to Margery Jourdemayne, and obtained from her magical charms and potions whereby she was able to win the love of the Duke of Gloucester, and so induce him to marry her. In 1430, Margery was arrested for sorcery, along with a certain Friar John Ashewell and a clerk named John Virley. All three were sent to Windsor and kept there in custody for some time; but their offence cannot have been considered very serious, since they were all released two years later, after finding someone to stand security for their future good behaviour. In Margery's case, it was her own husband who did this for her. She returned to Eye, and remained there, apparently practising her craft without disturbance, for the next nine years.

In 1441, when the case of the Duchess of Gloucester first came to light, she was one of those involved. The Duchess had no children and, ardently desiring a child, she had consulted Roger Bolingbroke and Canon Southwell. Margery Jourdemayne was also drawn into the affair. Between them, these three magicians fashioned a waxen figure, which the prosecution alleged was a representation of the young King, made to procure his death. The Duchess declared, in her defence, that it was altogether devoid of any murderous intent, and was simply meant to enable her to bear a child. There was nothing to show the truth of the matter, for such images could be used for many purposes, and might in this case have been made as well for the one end as for the other.

Bolingbroke, however, confessed that he had, at her request, used magical rites to ascertain the Duchess's future. He admitted that in doing so, he had 'presumed too far in his cunning', but he asserted most vehemently that there was nothing treasonable in this, and that all she wanted to know was what would happen to her, and to what rank she would rise. But for one so near the throne as she was, this simple question had a dangerous flavour, and might easily be construed, as it was in this case, as an enquiry into the length of the King's life and the possibility that her husband might succeed him. To the prosecution it was obvious that the visible image and the admitted divination were closely connected, and that they were parts of a serious conspiracy against the reigning monarch. Moreover, Canon Southwell had said Mass secretly in Hornsey Park over the instruments which Bolingbroke used in his ceremonies. He may, perhaps, have baptised the image also, in which case, the intention can only have been to harm the King, since the unborn child, the only other possible original of the puppet, had as yet no name.

Such perversion of holy things and ceremonies to the service of witchcraft was one of the blacker manifestations of mediaeval magic. It seems to have sprung in the first place from the conviction that spiritual power could be used equally well in either direction. For simple and ignorant people, it did not always appear sinful or blasphemous to employ it for mundane ends, if they were able to do so; but in the hands of the evil-minded this ancient notion opened the way to horrible parodies of religion and the twisting of sacred rites to purposes of murder and sacrilege. Sometimes an image, or a written charm, was hidden under the pall of the altar, so that the priest might unknowingly say Mass over it and thus endow it with spiritual strength that could be used thereafter against the chosen victim. More dreadful was the deliberate use of the sacred service itself to loosen evil forces. A renegade priest could recite the Mass for the Dead in the name of a living man, changing none of the words or rites, but only the intention. The victim, thus relegated to the shades before his time, died in a few days. The Mass of St Secaire sought much the same end, but more terribly; the service was altered to typify death and sterility and was celebrated at night in a ruined or deserted church. It does not appear in the records of English witchcraft trials, nor does the curious Gascon belief that whoever had the Mass of the Holy Spirit said for his intention could compel God to grant his desires, whatever they might be. Not infrequently the consecrated Host was stolen for magical purposes, such as use in love-charms, or to endow a thief with supernatural abilities. A faint echo of this idea was heard in Lincolnshire as late as last century, when the Vicar of Mumby was told by a girl in his parish that she had been advised to keep half the wafer from her First Communion in her pocket; if she did, she could become a witch and have miraculous powers. She hastened to assure the clergyman that she had not done so.[6]

When Bolingbroke was arrested, his instruments were seized with him, and on the afternoon of Sunday, 23 July, when he was forced to stand upon a high scaffold at Paul's Cross, they were displayed about him. He wore his conjuror's robes, 'wherein he was wont to sit when he wrought his necromancie', and in one hand he carried a magical sword, and in the other a sceptre. On the scaffold also was his painted chair, with swords at each of its four corners, from the points of which hung copper images. There were a variety of other very curious objects including, according to one account, a wax figure which was popularly supposed to be the disputed image of the King. Amongst all this, Bolingbroke was made to stand, exposed to the wonder and derision of the crowd, while a sermon was preached setting forth all his crimes.

There is no doubt that these were many and serious, though whether they included treason or not is impossible now to tell. The Duchess and her accomplices had, on their own admission, meddled with very dark powers, and practised divination, image-making, and the blacker forms of magic. What they all denied was any treasonable intent behind their actions. All four were condemned. Thomas Southwell was the most fortunate member of the little band, for he died in prison. Margery Jourdemayne was burnt at Smithfield. Bolingbroke was hanged, drawn, and quartered. His severed head was set up on London Bridge, and his four limbs sent to the four cities of Oxford, Cambridge, Hereford and York, there to be exposed as an awful warning to all other learned clerks who might be tempted to commit the same sin. The Duchess was condemned to do public penance on three separate occasions in London, walking bare-foot and bare-headed through the streets, and carrying a candle of two pounds' weight which she laid on the altars of the three churches that formed the goals of her melancholy pilgrimages. The rest of her life was passed as a prisoner, first at Chester, and afterwards at Peel Castle in the Isle of Man.[7]

Cardinal Wolsey was popularly supposed to have risen to power by sorcery, a belief that is perhaps understandable in view of his startling climb from a moderately low position to that of the highest in the land. In *The Practice of Prelates*, William Tyndale says 'he made by craft of necromancy graven imagery to bear upon him, wherewith he bewitched the king's mind, and made the king to dote upon him more than he ever did upon any lady or gentleman, so that now his Grace followed him, as he before followed the king'. Sir William Neville, brother of Lord Latimer, when applying to Richard Jones, a noted magician of Oxford, in the hope of learning his future, also asked him if it were not possible 'to have a ring made that should bring a man in favour with his Prince; seeing my Lord Cardinal had such a ring, that whatsomever he asked of the King's Grace, that he had'. Jones told him that he knew how to make such a ring, but when in 1532, he was examined on the matter, he denied that he had ever actually done so. Whether Wolsey did in fact possess such a talisman or not we do not know. His contemporaries believed in the efficacy of such things, and he may quite possibly have shared their belief sufficiently to have had one made for him by some of the numerous wisemen and conjurers who flourished in his time. But certainly, no ring ever fashioned by magician or demon was strong enough to bind the fickle favour of Henry VIII for long, and all the sorceries with which he was crecited could not save the Cardinal from ultimate disgrace when once he had offended his overbearing master.

The notorious Somerset trial of 1616 was concerned chiefly with the murder of Sir Thomas Overbury in the Tower of London, but it also revealed, in the course of evidence, many curious details relating to the practice of witchcraft in circles high and low in the preceding years. In 1606, Frances Howard, the beautiful and lively daughter of the Earl of Suffolk, was married at the age of thirteen to Robert Devereux, Earl of Essex, who was fourteen years old at the time. Youthful marriages of this sort were not at all unusual then. They were arranged customarily as a matter of polity between great families, and had, as a rule, as good a chance of success as any other. When the ceremonies and festivities were ended, the young couple separated and returned to their own families for three or four years, and then, their education or training finished, began their real married life together in their late teens. This was the pattern followed here, and certainly, neither bride nor groom can have had any inkling of the misery and evil that was to follow their perfectly normal wedding.

In 1609, the Earl of Essex came to the Court, where Frances then was, to claim his bride, as he had a perfect right to do. But in the meantime, she had fallen in love with the brilliant Robert Carr, the King's favourite, who later became the Earl of Somerset. She ardently desired his love, and she could not bear the idea of being united to any other man. 'The Countess of Essex', wrote Arthur Wilson in his *History of Great Britain* (1653), 'having her heart alienated from her husband, and set upon the Viscount,[8] had a double task to undergo, for accomplishing her ends. One was to hinder her husband from enjoying her; the other was to make the Viscount sure unto her.' In this difficult situation, she turned for help to two people known to be skilled in magic – Anne Turner and Dr Simon Forman.

The first was the pretty widow of a respectable doctor whom Frances had known for some time, in spite of the fact that her reputation since her husband's death was far from good. The other was Dr Simon Forman, of Lambeth. This man was an astrologer and an alchemist, and he was also a conjuror, who for many years practised magic more or less openly without interference from anyone. He died naturally in 1611, still unmolested by the authorities.

Through the arts of these two, Frances obtained the love of Robert Carr and, eventually, something far more deadly. For she was not content with a simple love-affair with the King's favourite; what she wanted was marriage. She persuaded Forman to make philtres and potions (and according to some accounts, a wax image), whereby the Earl of Essex was rendered impotent, and she was, therefore, able to bring a suit of nullity against him. She won it, and consequently was free to marry the Earl of Somerset on 26 December 1613. But not before Sir Thomas Overbury had been murdered, a crime of which she and Anne Turner were both suspected, and in the unravelling of which their former sorceries were brought to light.

Sir Thomas Overbury, formerly the very close friend of the Earl of Somerset, was strongly opposed to the latter's marriage with Frances Howard, and had been openly so all through the protracted nullity proceedings. She, perhaps not altogether unjustifiably, regarding him as her enemy. In 1613 he, being imprisoned in the Tower of London for refusing a foreign embassy offered to him, died inexplicably, apparently from poison. In 1616, Frances and Anne Turner were accused of this murder, and brought to trial, along with several others, including the Earl of Somerset, who was almost certainly innocent. He, his Countess, and Mrs Turner, were all three condemned. Mrs Turner was hanged as a murdress, but the other two, though equally found guilty of murder, were eventually pardoned, and left to live a quiet and obscure life together, very different from all that they had formerly known. It is possible that Mrs Turner had the best of it.

9 The White Witch

Since magic was essentially a neutral force, it could obviously be employed both for good and evil purposes – to save life as well as to destroy it, to heal as well as to waste the bodies of men and animals, to drive away plague, or harmful spirits, and to preserve the house from fire and storm instead of bringing these and other misfortunes down upon it. From very early times, householders and heads of families had largely relied for the protection of their homes and their farms upon a form of amateur magic which had been handed down to them through many generations of their forebears, and in which traditional rites and ceremonies could be performed at home without recourse to outside help. Most women knew a good many healing charms, some of them very ancient and rooted in paganism, and many were versed in the making of love-charms, or the best way of calling home an errant lover. They also knew how to keep away evil during the night, to prevent horses being 'hag-ridden', to protect the house from lightning, and the newborn child from fairies, and indeed, how to cope with almost every normal household peril or emergency. The farmer played his part in the magical observances that were absolutely essential at different seasons of the year, in the ancient charming of the earth and the plough, the kindling of need-fire, the crying of the neck and all the other rituals connected with Harvest-tide, and sometimes the offering of a necessary sacrifice when the murrain swept through the herds. Magical self-help of this kind lingered through many centuries, and only gradually faded into more or less meaningless superstition or mere custom. But there were always cases when home-made rites and charms, however time-honoured and trusted, were not enough to deal with some particular difficulty, and it was then that recourse was had to some local white witch, or wisewoman, or cunning-man.

Sometimes the person consulted was not really a white witch in the true sense of that term. Witches known to be malevolent could use their powers for benevolent ends at any time, if they wished, and very frequently, they did so. Many alleged witches were, in fact, two-sided in their customary practice, and were as well known for their healing or helpful charms as for any other kind of witchcraft. Agnes Sampson, of Haddington, who in 1591 was accused of taking part in the attempted murder by magic of King James VI of Scotland, was a noted wisewoman, constantly consulted by people of all sorts, before she fell into the hands of the Law. Anne Chattox who, along with her rival, Elisabeth Southerns, was the terror of Pendle Forest in the early seventeenth century, was willing to help her neighbours upon occasion, if they could muster the courage to ask her. A certain Dr Johnson, of Sunderland, told William Henderson that, in his childhood, he had known a witch named Nannie Scott. She apparently flourished in Sunderland at the beginning of the nineteenth century, and lived to a great age, dying quite peacefully at the end. In her hey-day, she told fortunes, and sold love-charms to those in need of them, and fair winds to sailors, or their wives. Children whom she took under her protection were said to be sure of good luck throughout their lives, but if any adult incurred her enmity, he or she stood in dire peril or an early death. She had a cat and a dog, both of them black and both extremely savage, which is not very surprising because, being taken for her familiars, the poor creatures were pelted and chased and mercilessly persecuted by the town's people. She was universally regarded as a black witch, and consequently feared, but this evil reputation did not prevent any one from turning to her for help in any serious difficulty. 'Few women', wrote Dr Johnson in a letter to Henderson, 'were more coaxed and toadied than was Nannie Scott.'[1]

There was, of course, always a certain danger in obtaining help from such sources. It was never really safe to have too close dealings with those who dabbled in dark waters, quite apart from the fact that to do so was condemned by the Church, both before and after the Reformation, and looked at askance by the Law. The true white witch was differently placed, for though he too used magic, he could not be justly accused of making any pact with Satan, or obtaining his knowledge by devilish means. Moreover, he could be trusted by those who sought his aid because his intentions were always – or nearly always – good. Occasionally, perhaps, he might stray across the very thin line that divided the black from the white, and indeed, while the witch-mania lasted, he was frequently suspected of doing so; but in general, he was accepted by most ordinary people as a safe friend, and a protector of the community in which he lived.

It is true that some of the sterner divines of the sixteenth and seventeenth centuries did not think of him thus. The fact that his arts were acknowledged to be magical was enough to condemn him in the eyes of those to whom all magic was an abomination stemming directly from the Devil. There were some for whom the good witch seemed to be a greater danger than the bad one because, by his helpfulness, he taught others to see virtue in forbidden spells and charms, and to turn to them readily in times of trouble. In his *Discourse on the Damned Art of Witchcraft* ... (1608), William Perkins wrote with bitter vehemence that

> by witches we understand not only those which kill and torment: but all Diviners, Charmers, Jugglers, all Wizards, commonly called wise men and wise women; yea, whosoever do anything (knowing what they do) which cannot be effected by nature or art; and in the same number we reckon

all good Witches, which do no hurt but good, which do not spoil and destroy, but save and deliver. . . . By the laws of England, the thief is executed for stealing, and we think it just and profitable: but it were a thousand times better for the land if all Witches, but specially the blessing Witch might suffer death. For the thief by his stealing, and the hurtful Enchanter by charming, bring hindrance and hurt to the bodies and goods of men; but these are the right hand of the Devil, by which he taketh and destroyeth the souls of men. Men do commonly hate and spit at the damnifying Sorcerer, as unworthy to live among them; whereas the other is so dear unto them that they hold themselves and their country blessed that have him among them, they fly unto him in necessity, they depend upon him as their god, and by this means, thousands are carried away to their final confusion. Death therefore is the just and deserved portion of the good Witch.

Doubtless, there were many others who thought along much the same lines, but this was not then, or at any other time, the opinion of the majority. Most ordinary people were content to judge a magician by what he did without troubling their minds too deeply about the sources of his powers. If he could, and would, help them when they needed help, that was good enough; and help them the true white witch did. He guarded his neighbours from spells cast upon them or their beasts by evil witches, and detected the source of enchantments already laid. He foretold the future, found lost or stolen goods, and detected thieves. He brought rain when it was needed, and helped to make the fields fertile; he enabled barren women to conceive, and cured both men and animals of the simpler ailments to which they were liable.

In the days when there were no qualified veterinary surgeons available, his services must have been of very great value to the farmer, since normally he had some genuine, if rather rough-and-ready veterinary skill which was hardly to be found elsewhere without great difficulty. So too, with human diseases and accidents, he brought to the patient's bedside a sound knowledge of herbal or animal remedies which were none the worse for being mixed up with spoken charms and incantations. The local wisewoman was usually the village midwife also, and not only performed the normal duties of that office, but gave the mother confidence by protecting her before she was churched, and the new baby before it was christened, from the perils of kidnapping fairies, or the subtle attacks of malicious witches.

The strong influence which many long-established wise-women or cunning-men were able to exercise over the people of their locality was often said to be due to fear, and so, in some cases, it may have been; but far more often it was due to the deep knowledge of the characters and circumstances of the villagers possessed by the magician, and the good sense and judgement which he (or she) very frequently brought to bear upon the problems they brought to him (or her). John Wrightson, who flourished in the late eighteenth and early nineteenth centuries, and was known as the Wise Man of Stokesley, was one of those who was both feared for his un-canny knowledge, and trusted because of his deep-seated wisdom. He himself claimed to know no more than the next man except when he was fasting; such gifts as he had were due to the fact that he was the seventh son of a seventh daughter but he would not, he said, be able to pass them on to his son when he died. Nor did he, though William Dawson, who claimed to be his successor, was said to be his nephew. He was widely consulted, especially in cases of animal-disease, stolen goods, and the need to know what was going on at a distance. Rather oddly (for his personal reputation was not particularly good), he was constantly asked to stand godfather to the local children, and at such christenings he normally appeared very gaily dressed in a scarlet coat and knee-breeches, white waistcoat, frilled shirt, and white stockings.

Tales of his exploits lingered all through North Yorkshire and South Durham long after his death. He always knew why he was needed before the messenger could tell him. Once, when a young bull was very ill, too weak to stand without the aid of ropes, Wrightson was sent for. He came, but at first seemed to take little interest in the case. At last, he strolled out to the byre, alone, and a few minutes later, the bull was seen to be standing up without any outside help, and eating heartily. It was quite cured, but no one ever knew how the cure had been effected.

Wrightson was very frequently asked to recover lost goods, especially in cases where theft was suspected. John Unthank, an old man of Danby, who had once known (and consulted) the Wise Man, told his Rector[2] that he always extracted a promise from the owner of the goods that no further action would be taken once they were restored. A miller on Esk-side missed a set of new weights, and applied for help to Wrightson. He was told to go home, where in due course he would find the weights, all covered 'wi' ass-muck' from the ash-midden where they were at that moment concealed. 'And', added the magician, sternly, 'thee's best not ask any questions. Ah kens all about it, and when thee gets the weights back, thee'll be none the worse. So, just hold thi' noise about the matter.' The miller did as he was told, and in a night or two, the weights mysteriously returned, covered with ashes as had been foretold, but quite unharmed. Their owner made no attempt to find out who the thief might be, whereby, no doubt, much bad feeling and bitterness in a small community was prevented. Rev. Mr Atkinson was of the opinion that the Wise Man's reputation was enough to drive any thief to restore the stolen goods, secretly and at once, as soon as he knew the magician had been consulted.

One last story about this remarkable man shows that he was credited with a sardonic sense of humour. Two young men on their way to the Hiring Fair at Stokesley thought it would be fun to 'have a bit of sport with Old Wrightson'. Accordingly, they went to his house, pretending to have come seeking his aid. The Wise Man received them civilly, seated them before the hearth and made up the fire. The day was cold, and at first the warmth was very grateful, but gradually it became rather too much. Presently the room was like a furnace, but their host, who was in a talkative mood, did not seem to notice it. The men tried to move away from the hearth, but found they were quite unable to do so. They could neither rise from their seats nor push back their chairs, and there they had to remain in great discomfort until the Wise Man suddenly released them with a contemptuous 'Good Night', and the advice to think twice another time before trying to 'make sport wi' Old Wrightson'.

Hodges, of Sedgeley, who practised his magical craft in the later seventeenth century, was a noted finder of lost property. He also had to power of showing the face of the robber in a mirror or other reflective surface. The Puritan divine, Richard Baxter, relates in his *Certainty of the World of Spirits* (1691) that when he was living in Kidderminster, one of his neighbours, having lost some yarn, sent to Hodges, some ten miles off, for help in recovering it, and was told that 'at a certain hour he should have it brought home again and put in at the window'. Baxter continues, 'and so it was; and as I remember, he showed him the person's face in the glass. Yet I do not think that Hodges made any known contract with the Devil, but thought it was an effect of art.'

In 1851, a curious tale was told to William Henderson by someone nearly connected with the matter. Shortly before he heard about it, a well-known wisewoman living in Leicester was approached by a poor woman and her daughter, both of whom were in great distress because they had been wrongfully accused of theft. A clergyman living in Rutlandshire had recently given a small party, and these two had been engaged to give extra help for the occasion. When the guests had all dispersed, a gold watch belonging to one of the inmates of the house was found to be missing. Careful enquiries were at once made, and the police called in, but the watch was not recovered, nor was the identity of the thief proved. Suspicion fell upon the two helpers from outside, though both had excellent characters, simply because it seemed impossible to suspect any of the guests or the resident servants.

Harassed by questioning and hurt by so much distrust, they begged the wisewoman to clear them somehow of this unjust accusation. She went into a trance and proceeded to describe, though without identification, first the Rutlandshire house, and then one of the guests at the party. This was a young girl who had been brought by a neighbouring clergyman and his wife, and was not previously known to her hosts of that night. This girl, said the wisewoman, went upstairs and entered one of the bedrooms, where a watch was hanging on a nail. She took it, hiding it in the front of her dress. She was now two miles away from the scene of the theft, still in possession of the watch, but already very frightened and anxious to be rid of it. As a result of this information, it was possible to trace the culprit to the vicarage where she was then staying. Her startled host was asked to make immediate investigations which, naturally, he was very unwilling to do, but finally, for the sake of the two women already accused, he was persuaded to act. He forced the girl to submit to a search, both of her boxes and of her person. The watch was found where she had first put it, and where the wisewoman had seen it – inside her dress.

Henderson records another and more tragic tale concerning a shepherd whom he had known himself, and from whom he heard the story shortly before the man died. When he first met him, this shepherd was hale and hearty, but, coming again to his cottage in the following Spring, he found the poor man apparently a complete wreck, lying wrapped in blankets on the settle by the fireside. It seems that in the previous autumn, he had developed acute rheumatism, and was unable to work. He went first to a doctor, but the treatment seemed to him to be too slow. Week after week passed without any improvement in his condition, and now to constant pain was added constant worry about money. He therefore, on the advice of his neighbours, turned to 'the Wise Man who lived far over the hills' for advice.

It is not at all clear that this man ever actually saw the shepherd, but having heard the details of his case, he said that desperate ills needed desperate remedies, and directed the patient's friends to wrap him in a blanket, and lay him in a 'sharp running stream'* that flowed not far from his cottage. This was done, although by now it was full winter. The sick man lay in the bitterly cold water for as long as he could endure it (about twenty minutes) and then entreated his friends to take him home. Naturally, he became very much worse as a result of this 'cure', and not long afterwards he died. Henderson does not record the name of the Wise Man, and perhaps he never knew it; but he firmly believed him to have been guilty of a heartless and cruel fraud, of which the unhappy shepherd was the victim. It is, however, quite possible that the Wise Man had acted in complete good faith, only that being perhaps rather ignorant, careless, and too much wedded to an ancient magical formula which he did not fully understand, he had attempted a cure beyond his natural skill and knowledge, with fatal results.[3]

Perhaps one of the most dangerous of the white witch's functions was the detection of other, evilly-disposed witches, to whose spells and incantations the misfortunes of his clients were

---

*It is possible, though Henderson does not mention it, that this 'sharp running stream' ran southwards, since south-running streams were usually thought to have curative powers, and water from them was often used in charms.

thought to be due. The Wise Man, on being asked by some agitated and frightened villager to say who it was that had cast a spell upon him, or upon his animals, rarely named any culprit outright; but he frequently predicted that the first person met or seen by the enquirer in a certain place, and at a certain time, would be the guilty individual. The afflicted person watched to see who would come, and was often very astonished by what he saw. Not infrequently, the first to arrive at the chosen spot was some totally innocent individual, going about his or her normal business, and only accidentally coming to that particular place at

the appointed time. Nevertheless, the encounter was often enough to draw down upon him lasting suspicion, and even open accusation of witchcraft, and sometimes immediate personal violence, or the lifelong enmity of some near neighbour.

A traditional charm for the detection of witches involved the ceremonial boiling of the nails, hair, and urine of the bewitched person, or the roasting of the heart of a beast that had supposedly been killed by spells, upon a very hot fire, at night, after having carefully shut every door and window in the house, and stopped up every chimney and aperture. It was usually believed that this charm would cause the witch to suffer agonising pain while the burning continued, and sometimes even to die from the effects of his sufferings. He (or she) would come to the house, begging for admission, and to be relieved of his agony, and thus his guilt would be proved. In another version of this charm, the end was less violent, but the witch was still drawn magically to the house, and being seen by those within, was known for what he was.

A Co. Durham story told in 1861 by a local clergyman relates how a farmer's wife came to him in great distress because she had been unjustly accused of witchcraft. Some neighbours lost two horses, and therefore consulted Black Willie, a wise man of Hartlepool, who told them to roast the pin-studded body of a pigeon on a fierce fire, and watch to see if anyone came near the house while this was going on. This they did, and saw the farmer's wife, who happened to be passing, on her own affairs, when no one else was about. Since then, she said, she had been considered a witch by every member of that particular family, and by everyone else to whom they confided the story. In Newcastle, another solitary nightfarer was more fortunate. A local wise man named Black Jock advised a farmer whose horse had died mysteriously to roast the animal's heart in the ritual manner between eleven and twelve o'clock at night, and promised him that he would then see the guilty man. The farmer did as he was told, and looking outside about midnight, he was aghast to see, approaching his house, one of the most highly respected and admired men in the district. Clearly, something was wrong here. This could not possibly be the culprit, and yet, so late at night, he could only be coming in answer to the charm. Next day, Black Jock was hastily summoned, and appeared to be as puzzled as his client. However, after a thorough search of the house, the mystery was solved. The doors, windows and other openings had all been properly closed, but one small hole on the stairs had been overlooked, and was still open to the outer air. Black Jock explained that this was quite enough to prevent the charm from working properly, and consequently no one had been drawn by it to the house that night. Thus, the reputation of the man seen approaching (who, as it turned out, had simply been on his way home, rather late), was saved, and so, in another way, was that of Black Jock.

Healers and charmers were of many different kinds. Some

who were generally called white witches were not really witches at all, since they did not consciously practise magic, but were simply the possessors of some peculiar gift. The seventh children of seventh children, and second-sighted men were often so-called, because the former had curative powers, and the latter the gift of foretelling the future, and seeing what was going on afar off. Yet, in fact, these abilities were congenital, not magical, and had nothing to do with witchcraft. Blacksmiths, because of their association with iron, fire, and horses, were supposed to be able to stop the flow of blood in men and animals and, in some cases, to exercise complete control over horses by means of the Horseman's Word.[4] Sometimes people with special names were supposedly able to cure some particular ailment, presumably by virtue of the power of the name. An old couple named Mary and Joseph, who lived at High Offley, in Staffordshire, at the end of the last century, were said to cure whooping-cough by giving the patient food from their table, without thanks or payment. In Cheshire, thirty years ago (and perhaps still), it was believed that the same ailment could be healed if the young person suffering from it received bread-and-butter from the hands of a woman whose maiden and married names were the same, though she had married a man to whom she was not related. Here, too, there must be neither thanks nor payment offered. But such people were not witches in the real sense, though they were often called so, and the intermittent help they could give from time to time was very different from that of the true magician.

Bridget Bostock, who lived in the eighteenth century at Church Coppenhall, in Cheshire, was in a rather more uncertain position. She was commonly called a white witch, though in fact she seems to have been an extremely devout woman, who performed her many cures by means of prayer and her own fasting spittle. At one period of her life, she suddenly became famous, and was visited by patients from near and far. A writer to the *Gentleman's Magazine* for 1748 says that she had been a healer of her neighbour's ills all her life, but that now, all of a sudden, her reputation had marvellously increased. She never took any payment for her cures, and she never broke her fast until the last person on any given day had been treated. 'She cures the blind', wrote the *Magazine* contributor, the deaf, the lame of all sorts, the rheumatic, King's evil, histeric fits, falling fits, shortness of breath, dropsy, palsy, leprosy, cancers, and, in short, almost every thing, except the French disease* which she will not meddle with, and all the means she uses for cure is, only stroking with her fasting spittle, and praying for them. . . . People come three score miles round. In our lane, where there has not been two coaches seen before these twelve years, now three or four pass in a day; and the poor come in cart loads. . . . So many people of fashion now come to her, that several of the poor country people make a comfortable subsistence by holding their horses. In short, the poor, the rich, the lame, the blind and the deaf, all pray for her and bless her, but the doctors curse her.

A curious instance of healing by prayer is mentioned by Mrs Leather in her *Folk-Lore of Herefordshire* (1912). Early in the present century, a horse was badly injured in the hunting-field. The haemorrhage was very great and could not be stopped, and the horse was in danger of bleeding to death. The owner was advised to send for a local blood-charmer, who lived not far off, and this he did. When the breathless messenger had explained what was wrong, the charmer withdrew a little way, and stood for a short time in an attitude of prayer; then returning to the messenger, he told him to go back to those who sent him, and he would find that the blood flow had stopped. The horse, said the charmer, would recover. The man made a note of the time, and went straight back to the scene of the accident, where as the charmer had said, he found that the haemorrhage had in fact ceased, and that this had happened precisely at the moment when the healer had told him it had. The horse recovered completely.

*Syphilis

'The gift of prophecy . . . was often highly dangerous'

10 Prophets and Astrologers

The gift of prophecy is rarely a comfortable possession, and, when witchcraft was a criminal offence, it was often highly dangerous. It is true that neither prophecy nor second sight are actually magical, since both are beyond the control of the person concerned. Either he has the questionable gift, or he has not; if he has it, he cannot help but see, and all that rests with him to decide is whether he will pass on the knowledge gained in this way, or keep it to himself. Even crystal-gazing and similar methods of deliberate enquiry into the future seem to demand some innate power in the scryer, for not everyone can do it, however carefully instructed, or willing to believe he may be. The old conception of a prophet as a man endowed with mystical gifts not derived from magic, and for which he was not personally responsible, has existed in every age, and it was this fact which no doubt gave him at all times so strong an influence, and caused so many wild utterances to be accepted as inspired truths. The seer might be holy, like the prophets in the Bible, or the early saints, or he might be quite the reverse; the essential thing for his hearers was that, for the time being at least, he was the lamp in which the fires of revelation burnt. Until he was proved to be wrong, he could always command a following, and in times of uncertainty or distress, his influence over the people was sometimes so great as to constitute a serious menace to the authorities.

Yet prophets were often confused with witches, and it is perhaps inevitable that this should be so, since witches also predicted the future. They were commonly supposed to do so by the power of the Devil, which the prophet was not; but in a universe crowded with demons, the strange was always suspect, and anything unusual might be the result of diabolic action. Even men of science, especially those whose work was in advance of the general ideas of their time, suffered on occasion from the suspicions of their more ignorant contemporaries. Roger Bacon in the thirteenth century gained a probably quite unmerited reputation for sorcery because of his scientific experiments, and was said to have constructed a magical head of brass, which spoke. The Oxford mathematician, Thomas Allen, who died in 1632, was looked at askance by many because he possessed some peculiar instruments, and also a watch, which was supposed to contain a devil. He had, says Aubrey,[1] 'a great many mathematical instruments and glasses in his chamber, which did also confirme the ignorant in their opinion'. Moreover, his servant, perhaps to indulge his own love of the marvellous, declared that he had seen spirits in the form of bees passing up and down his master's staircase in Gloucester Hall. Astrologers and scryers were even more open to suspicion than prophets, and both from time to time suffered the imputation, and occasionally the penalty, of witchcraft.

Authority at all times regarded prophets with hostility, whatever the source of their powers. In every age they tended to become centres of disaffection; their criticisms of Church or State were taken to be inspired utterances, no less than their predictions, and where their influences was strong, they could do an immense amount of harm. In 1562, a Lancashire fanatic from Manchester, who posed as the prophet Elias, created some considerable disturbance in London by his wild warnings of the wrath to come. He gained a number of followers, and was eventually condemned to stand in the pillory at Cheapside, and afterwards to be imprisoned in the Bridewell, where he died some three years later. Ten years before, a man named Clarke had been arrested for spreading 'certain lewde prophecies and slaunderous matters touching the Kinges Majestie and dyvers noble men of his Councell',[2] and so causing disaffection amongst

'A Lancashire fanatic . . . who posed as the prophet Elias'

Edward VI's subjects. Predictions as to the fate of kings and the identity of their successors were often the basis of treasonable plots, and incipient risings were sometimes encouraged by prophecies of their success. In her instructions to the Norfolk justices in 1554, Queen Mary I speaks of prophecies as 'the very Foundation of all Rebellion', and there is no doubt that most of her predecessors and some at least of her successors would have agreed with her.

To predict the date of the reigning monarch's death was treason, whether the prophecy sprang from an ecstatic vision or from divination. Those who did so might be tempted to hasten the event by more practical measures, or their associates might do it for them. Under Roman law, astrologers and necromancers who enquired into the length of the Emperor's ‚life were punished by death, and from early times, political prophets were liable to be beaten and driven from the city. In 1213, Peter the Wise, a Yorkshire hermit, was hanged because he foretold the melancholy end of King John's reign. The Elizabethan Act of 1580 states that

> . . . divers persons, wickedly disposed and forgetting their Duetie and Allegiaunce, have of late not only wished her Majesty's Death, but also by divers meanes practised and sought to knowe how long Her Highness should live, and who should reigne after her Decease, and what Changes and Alterations should thereby happen:

and then goes on to ordain that all who utter or print prophecies of the Queen's death, or conjure, cast nativities, and otherwise attempt to read the future shall 'suffer the paynes of Death'.

The uncertainty as to Elizabeth's successor and the troubled and changing times in which she lived were responsible for many such illegal divinations. In 1562, Arthur and Edmund Pole, and Anthony Fortescue, their brother-in-law, were charged with conspiring to depose and kill the Queen, and to place Mary Queen of Scots upon the throne. Associated with them in this conspiracy were two professed conjurors, John Prestall, who was related to the Poles, and Edward Cosyn. These two were accused of invoking evil spirits, and enquiring of these demons how their treasonable designs might best be carried out. The main defence of the other prisoners was that, while they had indeed plotted to place the Scottish Queen on the English throne, they had not intended any harm to Elizabeth. They had ascertained by conjuration that she could not possibly live after the end of the following spring, and they were prepared to wait until after her death for the success of their plans. They were all convicted and imprisoned in the Tower of London, being fortunate to have preserved their lives.

It is quite possible that the conspirators really believed that the

Queen would die soon, if Prestall told them so. He was a very well-known conjuror, and he seems also to have been something of an alchemist as well. In 1567, he offered to convert silver into gold, and was released from the Tower in consequence. Two years later, he is heard of in Scotland, producing gold and silver coins, though whether by alchemy or by counterfeiting is not clear. He seems to have been involved in more than one plot against the Queen, and it is somewhat surprising that his life should have been spared. At the time of the Pole conspiracy, there was no effective law against witchcraft and conjuring, for Henry VIII's Act of 1542 had been rescinded in 1547, and a Bill introduced in 1559 was lost because it had not been finally passed before the dissolution of Parliament in May of that year. In 1563, a new Witchcraft Act was passed which strictly forbade every kind of sorcery and enchantment, conjuring, and the invocation of spirits, as from 1 June of the same year. Prestall, however, had been guilty of more than conjuring and invocation, since he had taken active part in political plots, and the fact that he suffered nothing more serious than imprisonment is a proof of the Queen's clemency in such matters. In 1571, he was sentenced to death for treason, but Elizabeth reduced his punishment to imprisonment in the Tower. Twenty years later we hear of him at large in London, still practising magic and apparently unmolested, and eventually he disappears from recorded history.

Elizabeth suffered many magical attempts against her life. The Calendar of State Papers mentions 'Ould Birtles, the great devel, Darnally the sorcerer, Maude Two-good enchantress, the ould witch of Ramsbury', all of whom 'have diverse and sundry times conspired her life and do daily confederate against her'. In 1578, great excitement was caused by the discovery of three wax images buried in a stable. According to Mendoza, the Spanish Ambassador, who wrote an account of the affair to his own government, these figures were two spans high and covered with curious marks. The centre image had the word Elisabeth written on its forehead, the other two were dressed like royal coun-cillors, 'the left side of the images being transfixed with a large quantity of pigs' bristles as if it were some kind of witchcraft'.[3] It was instantly assumed that they were intended to cause the Queen's death, although Scot, in his *Discoverie of Witches*

(1584), says they were merely love-charms made by 'an old cousener, wanting money' for a young man who sought by this means to gain the love of three ladies. The need of money is understandable at all times, but why any young man should so diligently seek trouble as to attempt to secure the love of three women at once is not at all clear. Two years later, Nicholas Johnson, of Woodham Mortimer, was tried at Colchester Assizes for making a wax image of the Queen, and in 1589 a Mrs Dier was accused of conjuring against her. Strype, in his *Annals of the Reformation* (1709), says she could not be convicted because she merely 'spake certain lewd speeches tending to that purpose, but neither set figures nor made pictures'. Nevertheless, the case was considered sufficiently important for the records of her examination to be sent to Walsingham, and to the Queen's attorney, for consideration before she could be finally discharged.

Astrologers and alchemists were not, of course, magicians in the true sense, but their activities often resembled the magical, and were not always easily distinguishable from it. Both astrology and alchemy were ancient sciences which for centuries had attracted men of great learning, and also, inevitably, a certain number of charlatans who were drawn to them by the opportunities of fraud which they afforded to the quick-witted and the unscrupulous. Alchemists sought to transmute base metal into gold, not magically but by means of Natural Law, to find the Philosopher's Stone and the Elixir of Life, and to study and perfect the philosophy of the Natural World, which explained all things. Astrologers were concerned with the relation of the stars and planets to man, and their influence upon his fate and character. Their science, the forerunner of astronomy, and one of the most ancient in the world, required serious knowledge of the heavenly bodies and their movements; but the astrologer also foretold the future by the stars, sought auspicious dates for great events, cast horoscopes, and often invoked spirits. The step from this to real magic must have seemed, and perhaps was, a very short one, and it is not surprising that more than one astrologer fell under the suspicion of witchcraft. The uncertain position of such men in the spiritual world is mirrored in their great diversity of character and history, and their very varied treatment by the authorities, who sometimes persecuted them as magicians, and sometimes consulted them officially, and appointed them to positions of importance at Court, or in the Universities.

Henry VIII consulted astrologers about the sex of his coming child before the birth of Elizabeth, and, in 1559, Dr Dee was officially asked to find an auspicious date for that Queen's coronation. In the thirteenth century, Michael Scot, whose grave used to be shown at Burgh-under-Bowness, was court astrologer to the Emperor, as well as court physician. Cornelius Agrippa, the author of *De Occulta Philosophia,* was in the service of Margaret of Parma, and claimed to have been sent to London on a confidential mission from the Emperor Maximilian to Henry VIII. It was one of his doctrines that the study of magic was not bad, but good, because it enabled men to know more of God and the nature of the world in which they lived. Thomas Vaughan, brother of Henry Vaughan, the poet, seems to have thought along the same lines, for in *Magia Adamica* he says that 'magic is nothing but the wisdom of the Creator revealed and planted in the creature', and points out that the first men to adore Our Lord in this world were magicians. Vaughan was an Anglican clergyman who was driven from his living in Wales by Parliament because of his Royalist opinions. Like Dr Dee in the previous century, he saw nothing anti-Christian in his curious studies; for him magic was a philosophy 'not distasteful to the very Gospel itself'.

John Aubrey mentions two astrologers of his time, a Mr Marsh of Dunstable, and Dr Richard Nepier, Rector of Lynford, both of whom were men of piety and learning. Of the former, he says:

> . . . Mr Marsh did seriously confess to a friend of mine that astrology was but the countenance; and that he did his business by the help of the blessed spirits; with whom only men of great piety, humility and charity could be acquainted; and such a one he was.[4]

He was said to possess an old manuscript which had been found at Ashridge, near Berkhamsted, when that house was a monastery. It contained a number of strange receipts, including one that could be used to clear a house of evil spirits, by means of fumes. With this, it was claimed, he had freed several badly haunted houses.

Dr Nepier was both an astrologer and a physician, but, like Mr Marsh, he consulted spirits, of whom the chief was the angel Raphael. Amongst his papers, which Aubrey saw when they were in Elias Ashmole's possession, were many prescriptions and remedies, and against some of these were written the words 'R.Ris'. Ashmole said this stood for *Responsum Raphaelis*, the replies of the angel to questions put to him by the doctor. Through these answers, he was able to say with certainty whether any given patient would recover or die and, if the former, when he would be cured. He foretold his own death, which occurred on 1 April 1634, and correctly predicted in 1621 that Dr John Prideaux would be made a bishop twenty years later. When any patient came to him, he always withdrew into his closet to pray for a little while before he attempted to treat him. Aubrey says that 'his knees were horny with frequent praying', and his death came to him eventually while he was at prayer.

Not everyone trusted him, however, or believed that the spirit he most consulted was in fact an angel. Elias Ashmole told Aubrey how

> a woman made use of a spell to cure an ague, by the advice of Dr Nepier; a minister came to her, and severely reprimanded her for making use of a diabolical help, and told her she was in danger of damnation for it, and commanded her to burn it. She did so, and her distemper returned severely; inasmuch as she was importunate with the Doctor to use the same again; she used it, and had ease. But the parson hearing of, it, came to her again, and thundered hell and damnation and frightened her so that she burnt it again. Whereupon she fell extremely ill, and would have had it a third time; but the Doctor refused, saying she had contemned and slighted the power and the goodness of the blessed spirits (or Angels), and so she died.[5]

A man of very different character was Dr John Lambe, who was also a physician, and a consulter of spirits who were certainly not angels. He was undoubtedly guilty of criminal sorcery on more than one occasion, but he seems to have had a great gift of evading punishment. He was twice convicted at Worcester Assizes, the first time for 'wasting and consuming' Thomas, Lord Windsor, by witchcraft, the second for invoking evil spirits. Both these were capital offences, for which he should, by rights, have been hanged; but he was merely imprisoned, in Worcester to begin with, and later on, in London. There he remained for a considerable time, but his confinement was far from rigorous. He was exceedingly well treated, and was allowed to carry on his business as a physician, receiving the patients who came to him seeking health, and also other clients who came on rather less reputable errands. He seems to have lacked only his liberty, and even this he regained in 1624, when he was pardoned, and allowed to settle in his own house in London. He was known to the people of that town as 'the Duke's devil' because he enjoyed the powerful protection of the Duke of Buckingham, and is said to have taught him the magical arts. A violent storm of thunder and lightning, rain and hail, which burst over London on 12 June 1626, just as the House of Commons was considering impeachment proceedings against Buckingham, was popularly supposed to have been raised by Dr Lambe. Two years later, in 1628, this strange man who had escaped execution for so long, came to a sudden and terrible end. As he was returning from the Fortune Theatre in Golden Lane, the London mob, which detested both him and his ducal patron, fell upon him without warning, and literally beat him to death.

One of the most famous English students of the secret arts was Dr John Dee, a man of deep learning and of sincere goodness. He was born in 1527, in London, and studied in his youth both at Cambridge and at Louvain. He was already extremely interested in astronomy before he went to the latter university, and there he extended his studies to include mathematics and natural philosophy, astrology and alchemy. In 1550, when he was twenty-three, he left Louvain with a reputation for learning so firmly established that he attracted great crowds to his lectures in Paris, and was offered a professorship in mathematics at the College de Rheims. He was also asked to go with the French Embassy to Turkey, but he declined both invitations because he wanted to get back to England. In 1551, he was presented to Edward VI, and was afterwards awarded a pension of one hundred crowns a year. This, though not in orders, he afterwards commuted for the rectorship of Upton-on-Severn.

Four years later, in 1555, he suffered a misfortune which might have meant the end of his career, had his judges been less intelligent. He was accused, along with three other men, of calculating the nativity of Queen Mary, Philip of Spain, and Princess Elizabeth, and also of plotting to kill the Queen by magic or by poison. George Ferrys, one of the accusers, added

Dr Dee

a charge of keeping familiars, and added point to his statements by declaring that no sooner had he laid the charges than one of his children died and another went blind. In view of Dee's known character, these accusations were wildly improbable, at least as far as plotting against the Queen's life or injuring the Ferrys children were concerned. He had, however, gained an undeserved reputation as a magician very early in his career, because of his curious studies and writings, and this reputation was to pursue him throughout his life. What seems to have happened in this instance was that some member of Princess Elizabeth's household approached him about a horoscope, a legitimate matter for an astrologer's consideration, but dangerous in the particular circumstances of the time, having regard to the fact that Elizabeth was next in succession to the throne. The case was tried by the Star Chamber, and Dee was acquitted of high treason. His religious views, which had also been called into question by George Ferrys, were examined by Bishop Bonner and found to be quite satisfactory.

In Elizabeth's reign, Dee was more fortunate, for the Queen befriended him at intervals throughout her life. He was asked to find an auspicious date for her coronation; when Halley's Comet appeared in 1577, he was summoned to Windsor and remained there for three days, explaining its purely natural origin. On another occasion, when a pin-studded image was found in Lincoln's Inn, he was again called in to assure the Queen that it could do her no harm. In 1578, he sent to Frankfurt-on-Oder to consult with certain physicians there about the Queen's health, she being troubled with rheumatism at the time. Although she did not give him the important post for which he hoped, she made him presents of money from time to time, and visited him at his house in Mortlake. After the publication of his *Monas Hieroglyphica,* she is said to have become his pupil, and whether this was actually so or not, she does seem to have taken an interest in his writings, and to have asked him to explain them to her.

John Dee's intellectual curiosity was at all times enormous, and there is little doubt that the occult interested him more than anything else, in spite of his great learning in other directions. But he was not a witch, and he bitterly resented his own all too firmly established reputation as a magician. In the Preface which he wrote to Henry Billingsley's translation of Euclid's Elements in 1571, he complains of the injustice he suffers from those who think of him as 'a companion of Helhounds, and a caller and a conjuror of wicked and damned spirits'. His difficulty was that he did desire to converse with spirits, and sought by numerous experiments to do so, and if he did it only in the interests of pure knowledge, and without any loss of religion, that was, unluckily, rather more than most ordinary individuals of his time could understand.

In 1581, when he was already fifty-four years old, he turned to crystal-gazing. This ancient form of divination was commonly practised to detect thieves, discover the whereabouts of absent friends, or predict the future, but Dee used it to put himself in communication with spirits. He heard of a scryer named Barnabas Saul, who was not only well versed in the art, but was also a preacher, and a man of good reputation. This last was important, for the doctor desired to call only good spirits, and it was believed in some quarters that only the pure of heart could see them. For this reason, young children were sometimes employed as scryers. Thus, in 1467, William Byg (or Lech), accused of sorcery in the Archbishop of York's court, confessed that he had, for several years, discovered thieves and found stolen goods by means of the crystal. As, however, he could not see anything himself in the glass, he employed a small boy, under twelve years of age. This child was required to say certain Latin prayers, and to call upon God to send three angels from a right-hand direction, to reveal the true answer to his enquiries. Then he had to peer into the crystal, wherein he saw visions, sometimes of the angels themselves, and sometimes of the thieves sought for or the places where the stolen goods were hidden.

Like Byg, Dr Dee was not able to scry himself, so he invited Saul to do so for him. He was told that the Angel Annael had appeared in the crystal, and had answered the various questions put to him. On another occasion, Saul declared that, when sleeping in Dee's house at Mortlake, he was greatly troubled about midnight by some sort of 'spiritual creature'. Later, however, he confessed that this tale was untrue, and eventually, it became clear that he was, in fact, an imposter. He left Mortlake, and it was after his disgrace that Edward Kelly, that curious creature with whom Dee was destined to work for so long, first appeared on the scene.

Kelly's real name was Talbot, and he is so called in the earlier entries concerning him in Dee's diary. He was born in Worcester in 1555, and was apprenticed to a chemist there. He seems to have had a considerable knowledge of chemistry, and also claimed to be versed in astrology; he certainly attempted necromancy at least once before he came to Mortlake in 1582. John Weever, in his *Ancient Funerall Monuments* (1631) describes how he

> . . . upon a certain night in the Park of Walton in le dale, in the County of Lancaster, with one Paul Waring (his fellow companion in such deeds of darkness), invocated some one of the Infernall Regiment, to know certain passages in the life, as also what might be known of the Devil's foresight of the manner and time of the death of a noble young gentleman, as then in wardship. The black ceremonies of the night being

'. . . *upon a certain night in the Park of Walton in le dale*'

ended, Kelley demanded of one of the gentleman's servants what corse was last buried in Law churchyard, a church thereto adjoyning, who told him of a poor man that was buryed there but the same day. He and the said Waring intreated the foresaid servant to go with them to the grave of the man so lately interred, which he did; and withal did help them to dig up the carcase of the poor caitiff, whom by their incantations they made him (or rather some evil spirit through his organs) to speak, who deliver strange predictions concerning the said gentleman.

Weever adds; 'I was told thus much by the said serving-man, a secondary actor in that dismal abhorred business; and divers gentlemen and others now living in Lancashire to whom he related this story.'

In 1582, Kelly presented himself at Dee's house in Mortlake, having been for some time an itinerant astrologer. He confessed later that he had been sent there (though he did not reveal by whom) to entrap the doctor into an acknowledgement of dealings with the Devil, but came to the conclusion that it would pay him better to stay and work upon his credulity. In spite of his decidedly shady character, Kelly really seems to have had some skill as a scryer, and to have believed in his own powers. Af his first seance with Dee, he saw the angel Uriel, who told him to make a Holy Table and a Seal of God for the better carrying-out of their work. After this, seances, or 'actions' took place almost daily; St Michael was seen, and a child-angel who brought what Dee called a 'shew-stone' for their use. Kelly saw and described the visions, and Dee recorded them. Meric Casaubon, who edited the doctor's account of what took place,[6] says that Dee would never consent to speak with any but known good spirits, but some of the later manifestations were sufficiently remarkable, and very different from the first angelic appearances.

A month after the sittings began, St Michael ordered Kelly to take a wife and, though very unwilling to do so, he obeyed soon afterwards, marrying a young girl from Chipping Norton named Joan Cooper. This marriage was never very successful. Dr Dee's own wife probably deplored the angel's interference also, as it meant that she had to endure the constant presence in her house, not only of Kelly whom she never really trusted, but also of his young wife. With domestic discord in his home and steady pressure from his creditors outside, Dee's life at this time cannot have been very happy. Much later, when both couples were together in Bohemia in 1587, the spirit Madini suggested that the two men should have their wives in common. They were greatly perturbed, as well they might be, but after consulting with another spirit, they decided to obey this very peculiar command. The women, however, were less docile and demanded further consultations, declaring the suggestion to be contrary to the laws of God, and intensely distasteful to themselves. Whether the idea really came from Madini, as Kelly declared, or from himself, is not at all clear, but certainly the scryer was anxious to carry it out, and at last persuaded the others to sign with him a document which ran: 'I John Dee, Edward Kelly and our two wives covenanted with God, and subscribed the same, for indissoluble and inviolate unities, charity and friendship keeping between us four, and all things between us to be common, as God by sundry means willed us to do.' What the result of this strange agreement was is unknown, for Dee says nothing further about it in his account of his spiritual adventures.

The two astrologers and their wives travelled extensively in Europe, first as the guests of Albert Laski, a Polish prince who visited the doctor at Mortlake and took part in seances there, and afterwards in Thuringia, Hesse-Cassel, and Bohemia. At one period, the Papal Nuncio succeeded in having them banished from the Emperor's dominions as magicians, but through the favour of Count Rosenberg, this sentence was partially remitted, and they were allowed to live in any part of Rosenberg's territory. Here Kelly practised alchemy, and is said to have produced gold. Later on, he was sufficiently restored to the Emperor's favour to be made a knight, and in his later writings, Dee usually refers to him as Sir Edward.

But in spite of the spirit-inspired agreement of 1587, the strange friendship was not destined to last much longer. In 1589, Kelly secured employment for himself, and the double household broke up. The scryer had only another four years to live, and two of these were spent as a prisoner in Pirglitz Castle, after being accused of conspiracy against the Emperor. He was freed on the request of Queen Elizabeth, but remained in Bohemia; on 25 November 1595, Dee noted briefly in his diary that Sir Edward Kelly was dead. Dee himself returned to England, and in the year of Kelly's death, he became Warden of Manchester College. He made some further attempt at scrying, but could not find any one as skilled as Kelly to help him. In 1604, he was evidently once again troubled by his own reputation for sorcery, or perhaps feared persecution, in view of the new Witchcraft Act then being debated in Parliament. He petitioned King James to have him 'tryed and cleared of that horrible and damnable, and to him most grievous and dammageable sclaunder ... that he is, or hath been a conjuror or caller or invocator of divels'. The King did not grant his request, but neither did he trouble him in any way, and four years later, the aged astrologer died peacefully in his house at Mortlake where he had made so many strange experiments, and struggled with so many domestic and financial difficulties.

A humble follower in the great doctor's footsteps was Thomas Light, who lived at Walton, near High Ercall in Shropshire, in the early years of the nineteenth century. He possessed a copy of *The Theomagia of John Heyden, Gentleman,* an astrological work published in 1662 in which the author claimed to set forth 'the occult powers of Angels, of Astromancy, the Knowledge of the Rosie Crucian Physicke, and the Miraculous Secrets of Nature'. With its aid, Light invoked spirits, consulted the stars, and satisfied the varied needs of his neighbours and clients. His advice was sought by people from as far away as Staffordshire, Cheshire, and Wales, and not by the illiterate and superstitious alone. He cured the sick, found stolen goods, told fortunes, and charmed cocks for cock-fighting. Like Dr Nepier, he always retired into an inner room when his clients first arrived, and there consulted the spirits on their case; sometimes he could be heard wrestling with supernatural powers, like Jacob at the Ford of Jabbok. When he died, he left a considerable amount of money to a nephew and a niece, but his cherished book passed into the hands of a Birmingham bookseller, and so away from the family.

At a slightly later period, an astrologer named Rawlinson lived at Roe Green, in the Township of Worsley, in Lancashire. He was employed by the Bridgwater Trust as a gaffer, or overseer, and remained with the Trust until his death. In his leisure hours, he studied astrology and charmed the diseases of his neighbours. He possessed two crystals, with which he predicted the future, and told fortunes, and he also had half a dozen astrological works, including Lilly's *Christian Astrology.* On stated dates, he used to go to Manchester and there meet other astrologers in a quiet public-house. They gathered behind locked doors in an upper room, and sometimes remained deliberating there for hours together. 'Owd Rollison', as he was widely known, lived to a ripe old age, and left behind him several sons and a daughter; but like Light, with his nephew and niece, he was not able to transmit to any of his children his own deep interest and desire for occult knowledge.

11 The Decline of Belief

Every passionate assertion calls forth some contradiction, and every firmly-held creed knows at least some doubters and some sceptics. The witchcraft belief was no exception. Even when it was at its height, there were always a few who questioned it, and others who, while they accepted the existence of magic and the possibility of spirits intervening in human affairs, yet doubted whether quite so many people were given to sorcery as contemporary accusations and the following trials seemed to show, or whether that crime was, in fact, the explanation of almost every serious disaster or disease. In 1563, Johan Wier, physician to the Duke, of Cleves, suggested in his *De Praestigiis Daemonum* that witchcraft was more a matter for physicians than for theologians and magistrates. He believed that the witches themselves were often subject to delusions, and that their alleged victims were as frequently sufferers from diseases due to natural causes as from those due to spells. Wier was an earnest student of demonology, and credited Satan and his followers with very extensive powers of interfering with human beings. He did not think, for instance, that witches actually attended Sabbats, or that they rode through the air, or actively bewitched their neighbours and the latter's beasts, but rather that the Devil made them think that they did so. Where their intentions were evil, they deserved punishment, but in so far as they were themselves deluded, they were not entirely sane, and were not, therefore, really responsible for all their actions. This was a humane and reasonable view, very far from widespread in his time; and it was partly to refute such strange and unwelcome opinions as these, and those of Reginald Scot which followed them in 1584, that King James I wrote his own book on witchcraft in 1597.

Scot was a Kentish squire who knew his countrymen very well. In his *Discoverie of Witchcraft* (1584), he went rather farther in disbelief than Johan Wier, though, like him, he acknowledged the existence of evil spirits. He claimed, however, that little was known about them, and that most of the strange events ascribed to them were really due either to conscious human fraud, or to delusion. He believed that criminal witches could sometimes achieve their ends by secret poisoning, but in their magical or demon-aided powers, he had no faith whatever. That large numbers of ordinary, simple people were devoted to harmful magic, or to the worship of the Devil, was altogether too much for his common sense and in his book he said so, boldly and clearly.

Wier and Scot were both Protestants, but such doubts as they experienced were not confined to men of their faith. In 1631, Friedrich von Spee published his *Cautio Criminalis,* a passionate and reasoned protest against false accusations of witchcraft and the useless torture of prisoners. Von Spee was a Jesuit who had seen many witch trials in Germany, and acted as confessor to many accused persons. Like Remy and Bòdin, he had heard the evidence and wrote of what he knew; unlike them, he was driven by his knowledge, not to greater severity but to the unhappy conclusion that most of the condemned and tortured prisoners had been innocent of the crimes for which they suffered. He did not doubt that sorcery was possible or that witches lived and flourished, but he could not believe that all the miserable wretches whom he had seen were in fact witches. He regarded the general readiness to credit the most revolting forms of evil as something which blackened the face of religion everywhere, and thrust men back into that very paganism which they imagined themselves to have uprooted. In the last chapter of his book he remarks, bitterly:

> Incredible are the superstition, the envy, the slanders and backbitings, the whisperings and gossip of the common people in Germany, which are neither punished by magistrates nor reproved by preachers. These are the causes that first rouse suspicion of witchcraft. All the punishments of divine justice with which God has threatened men in his Holy Scriptures are held to come from witches. God and nature no longer do anything – witches everything. Hence it is that all demand, with violent outcry, that the magistracy shall proceed against the witches, whom only their own tongues have made so numerous.[1]

Forty-six years later, in 1677, John Webster published his *Displaying of Supposed Witchcraft* in which, amongst other things, he related the story of his encounter with Edmund Robinson, when that young liar was being taken round the countryside, supposedly detecting witches. Webster had been many things in his time, including a well-known preacher, and a physician. The main object of his book was to refute the works of Casaubon and Glanvil, both of whom were firm believers in the satanic origin of witchcraft. Webster did not deny that there were witches, and that they could, and did, work evil, but he considered that they did this by their own knowledge and application of natural laws, and not by the help of the Devil. In his account of the Black Assizes at Oxford, for instance, he ascribes to Roland Jenks a knowledge of poisons and chemistry far greater than that unlucky prisoner probably possessed.

In 1577, a fearful outbreak of typhus occurred in Oxford during what was afterwards known as the Black Assizes. Not only the prisoners, but also judge, witnesses, jury-members and lawyers were infected, and so were very many of the townsfolk. Two main theories were put forward at the time to explain the disaster. One was that it was due to a poisoned 'damp', or vapour, arising from the prisoners themselves, or from the soil. The other was that it was caused by the sorcery of Roland Jenks, a Catholic bookseller then in prison for selling seditious literature. This man is said to have moulded a secret and magical candle which, when lit, raised the plague. In his account of the affair, Webster also blames Jenks, but not his devil-aided magic. He says the man possessed some rare and little-known poisons which, when slowly burnt, could be used to raise dangerous vapours. From these perilous materials he had made a candle, and had lit it as soon as he was condemned. The result was a violent and unexpected outburst of the pestilence.

Webster's views on this and other particular cases did not denote that he had no faith in witchcraft as such. Like James I, he was a believer in principle, but frequently a doubter in practice. He tells his readers, very firmly, that

> I do not thereby deny either the Being of Witches, nor other properties that they may have, for which they might be so called; no more than if I deny that a dog hath rugibility (which is proper only to a Lion), doth it follow that I deny the being of a Dog, or that it hath latrability.

But he did deny that witches commonly made visible and corporeal contracts with the Devil, or were transformed into cats and dogs and other animals, or could fly through the air, or had the power to raise storms. Such crimes as they committed were accomplished by 'meer natural means', and in his Dedication, he urges magistrates to reject all impossible confessions, and to distinguish carefully between impostors and those deluded people who mistakenly imagined themselves to be witches.

James I's sceptical turn of mind provided a strong impetus, if not to disbelief, at least to caution in the conduct of witch-trials during his reign. His sharp rebuke to Sir Humphrey Winch and Sir Randolph Crew at Leicester in 1616 impressed his other judges and made them anxious to avoid similar trouble for themselves, while his own investigations demonstrated how very easy it was for the unduly credulous to be deceived by imposters. For James, supposedly bewitched persons were not the objects of instant sympathy that they were for so many of his subjects; they might just as easily, and in his view more probably, be guilty of fraud, or, at best, be victims of delusion. When Anne Gunter, of North Moreton, in Berkshire, began to have hysterical fits in 1604, she accused three local women of bewitching her. In the following year, the case came to the notice of King James, and he examined her, first in Oxford, then in Windsor, where the accused women were imprisoned, and later on in Whitehall. He caused her to be treated by Dr Edward Jorden, who was a specialist in hysterical troubles. The King came to the conclusion that the girl was lying, as the physician did also, and he urged her to tell the full truth, promising that if she did so, no harm would come to her. She then admitted that all her symptoms of possession had been feigned, and her entire story false. She had, she said, acted under the instructions of her father who, like Edmund Robinson's father, sought by this means to revenge himself upon a neighbour[2]. Nor was this the only case of its kind with which the King was involved. Dr Fuller, in his *Church History of Britain* (1655) speaks of his skill in detecting impostures, and mentions (though he does not name), a girl who suffered regularly from fits, supposed to be induced by witchcraft. These fits came upon her every day at the same hour, until the King began to visit her, when, says Fuller, she, 'loath to be so unmannerly as to make His Majesty attend her time, antedated her Fits many hours, and instantly ran through the whole Zodiac of tricks which she used to play'. The King, we gather, was not impressed. Such cases only served to confirm to him that fraud was all too common, and he never ceased to urge his judges to be exceedingly circumspect when dealing with prisoners committed for trial on the evidence of supposedly bewitched persons.

In 1622, Edward Fairfax, of Fewstone, in Yorkshire, accused six women of afflicting his two daughters with fits over a period of several months. The children declared that their persecutors met at Timble Gill and feasted with the Devil at midnight, the food being provided and cooked by one of the witches who sat at the table-foot, while the Devil sat at the head. On one occasion, Helen Fairfax was found wandering alone on the moors some way from her home, and said she had been carried there by one of the band, and had seen a number of women gathered round a huge fire. These tales, and their accompanying fits and trances, convinced the harassed father that his children were the victims of sorcery, and he duly accused the women before the justices. Further support was given to the charge by John Jeffray, a neighbour, who came forward to declare that his own child, Maud, was also bewitched. When the hearing opened at York, the three little girls were brought into the court, and promptly fell into a trance as soon as they saw the prisoners. They were carried out unconscious, and left in another room to recover. But Sir George Ellis and the other justices, mindful of King James' warnings, were not easy in their minds. They left the court-room, and questioned the children, as soon as these had recovered their senses. In a short time they returned, with the news that Maud Jeffray had confessed that her fits were simulated, and that she had only accused the women concerned by order of John Jeffray, her father. Later on, she denied that she had made this confession, but her father was sent to prison, and his charge against the women dismissed. The little Fairfaxes confessed nothing, and did not appear to be counterfeiting their fits. In their case, the trial of the prisoners went on, but the evidence against them was insufficient, and the proceedings were stopped. No one doubted Edward Fairfax's complete honesty; he was pronounced guiltless of fraud, and the wild stories told by his hysterical little girls were, probably correctly, laid at the door of the Jeffrays. Fairfax writes in his account of the matter that when all was over, it was given out that 'Jeffray and his family devised the practice, to which they drew my eldest daughter, and she the younger'.[3]

The famous case at Bury St Edmunds in 1664 might have ended in the same way, had the two women concerned had another judge. Sir Matthew Hale was one of the ablest judges of his time, a conscientious seeker after truth, and a compassionate and humane man. He was, however, a firm believer in witchcraft, and in his summing-up at this trial, he gave the jury a very strong lead, telling them that he had no doubts at all as to the existence of witches, for not only did the Scriptures affirm it, but 'the wisdom of all Nations had provided Laws against such Persons, which is an Argument of their confidence of such a Crime'. That even a man of his known wisdom should hold such beliefs was not at all surprising at that time; what is perhaps strange is that he did not consider more carefully the possibility of fraud, particularly as in this case it was brought to his attention by Sergeant Keeling, who had satisfied himself that his own suspicions were correct. Sir Matthew, however, was not impressed, and in his summing-up, merely urged the jury to consider the evidence carefully, but did not review it for them, or make any reference to Keeling's allegations of imposture.

The prisoners were Amy Duny and Rose Cullender, two women of Lowestoft, who were reputed to be witches in their own town. This reputation they seem to have strengthened by frequent displays of bad temper, and by injudicious threats. They were brought to trial at Bury St Edmunds on a charge of bewitching a number of little girls, with whose parents they had quarrelled for rather trivial reasons. Samuel Pacy alleged that his daughters, Elisabeth and Deborah, aged eleven and nine respectively, had suffered from violent fits ever since the two witches had come to his house, to buy herrings, and had been refused. The children constantly cried out that the women were in the room with them, and that they sent their imps to torment them. In consequence, they sometimes lost the use of their limbs, or were struck dumb; occasionally they vomited pins and nails, as many as thirty at a time, though their aunt, Margaret Arnold, to whose care they had been sent, declared she had carefully concealed all the pins in the house. Once Deborah brought up a twopenny nail with a broad head, and said that 'a thing like a bee' had forced it into her mouth. Both children claimed that they saw mice constantly running up and down their aunt's house in Yarmouth, though these were invisible to everyone else. Once Elisabeth crept under a table and there caught a mouse, or so she said. She threw it on the fire, and it exploded with a flash like gunpowder. Her aunt saw the flash, but she had to admit that she had seen nothing in the child's hand. The care of two children so bewitched can have been no rest cure, and we can only hope that poor Mrs Arnold was adequately rewarded by their parents.

Edward Durent similarly complained that his little girl, Ann, began to suffer from fits and stomach-pains and pin-vomiting soon after his wife had refused to supply Rose Cullender with herrings. Evidence of like nature was brought by the parents of little Jane Bocking, and the eighteen-year-old Susan Chandler. In addition, a certain John Soam swore that Rose Cullender had bewitched his cart so that it could be neither moved nor unloaded, and so had remained until the following day.

When the trial opened at Bury St Edmunds, Elisabeth Pacy, Ann Durent, and Susan Chandler were brought there to give evidence. They were all apparently in good health when they arrived, but as soon as they entered the court-room, their fits came upon them, and they were unable to speak rationally or give proper testimony during the proceedings. Elisabeth lost all power of movement, and lay for some time upon a table in a semi-conscious condition. When she had recovered a little, Amy Duny was made to touch her, and the child immediately sprang up and scratched the witch's face, refusing to stop until she was dragged away by force. Susan Chandler also fell into a fit at the sight of Rose Cullender; when asked if she had anything to say against either prisoner, her only reply was a repeated shriek of 'Burn her! Burn her!

The accused women denied all the charges brought against them, nor did they ever acknowledge anything, even after it was alleged that the Devil's Mark had been found on Rose Cullender. The great Dr (afterwards Sir Thomas) Browne, then one of the leading scientific men of his time, was asked what he thought about the children's seizures, and whether they could be caused by witchcraft or not. He replied that, in his view, 'the Devil in such cases did work upon the Bodies of Men and Women, upon a Natural Foundation, (that is), to stir up and exicite such humours super-abounding in their Bodies to a great excess', and added further that 'he conceived that these swouning fits were Natural, and nothing else but what they call the Mother,* but only heightened to a great excess by the subtilty of the Devil, co-operating with the Malace of these which we term Witches, at whose Instance he doth these Villanies'.

These views, from so learned a man, naturally carried great weight, and must have had a very considerable influence on the jury. There were, however, some dissentient voices. Mr Sergeant Keeling was not satisfied with the evidence, and declared roundly that if such evidence was to be accepted, no one was safe. He believed that the children were acting, and along with

*Hysteria

Lord Cornwallis and Sir Edmund Bacon, he demanded a practical test. A bewitched person was commonly supposed to react violently to the touch, or even the presence, of the witch, and, naturally, to be unaffected by those of any one else. Hence, it was arranged for one of the children to be taken, blindfolded, into a room where Amy Duny was. She knew the witch was there because she had been told, but she could not see her movements or those of any other person. A bystander touched her, and she, assuming it was Duny, immediately fell into a fit. For Sergeant Keeling and those with him, this was enough; they had been 'unsatisfied' before, and now they 'did believe that the whole transaction of this business was a meer imposture.'[4] Nevertheless, in spite of what appeared to be clear evidence of cheating on the part of at least one of the children, the judge was unconvinced, and summed up heavily against the prisoners. Both women were condemned and, in due course, hanged.

In the story of English witchcraft, Sir John Holt bears a justly honoured name. He brought to every trial a mind unclouded by prejudice, and a single-hearted desire to give the prisoner every chance. Throughout his career, he showed to all accused persons, whatever their crimes, a wide humanity that was all too uncommon in his day, and Sir Richard Steele tells us in *The Tatler* that every prisoner brought before him knew, 'though his spirit was broken with guilt and incapable of language to defend itself, all would be gathered from him which could conduce to his safety, and that his judge would wrest no law to destroy him, nor conceal anything to save him'. He was quite unaffected by the witchcraft mania, and he did not believe, as did so many of his contemporaries, that to acquit a witch was to undermine the constitution or deny revealed religion. In the eleven sorcery trials over which he presided, he never failed to secure the discharge of the accused person, and his impartial common sense did much to hasten the decline of the witch-belief throughout the country.

He was born at Thame in Oxfordshire in 1642, and became Lord Chief Justice of the Court of King's Bench in 1689, a position which he held until his death in 1710. In his youth, he was a wild young man, and left his University (Oxford) without a degree. There is an interesting story about this period, which had its repercussions on his later career as a judge. Once, in an alehouse near Oxford, he found himself without money to pay his bill. His landlady had a daughter who suffered from ague, so he offered to square his reckoning by curing her. He scribbled a few words of Latin on a piece of parchment, told the girl to wear it on her wrist, and departed on his way rejoicing. Many years later, when he was a judge, a woman was brought before him, charged with curing fevers magically by means of a written charm. This charm was produced, and handed to the judge for inspection; but he had seen it before. It was the same piece of parchment which he had once used to extricate himself from an awkward predicament, and the prisoner, though he had not recognised her immediately, was the woman to whom he had given it. It had, she said, cured her daughter of the ague, and thenceforward she had used it to heal others. By a stroke of extraordinary good fortune, she had been brought before the one judge in England who knew its history, and was not afraid to tell the truth about it, and, in consequence, the charge against her was dismissed.

In 1702, a case was tried by Holt which is of interest mainly because it shows how very slow ordinary people then were to accept the innocence of any accused witch, even after he or she had been acquitted in the courts. Richard Hathaway, a black-smith's assistant in Southwark, suffered from fits, and said he was bewitched by Sarah Murdock, a local waterman's wife. He tried to break the spell by springing on her from behind when she was taking down her shutters one morning, and scratching her face till the blood ran down. The cure so affected was apparently only temporary, for some time later, he and some friends went once more to the house and scratched the unhappy woman again. He then charged her before Sir Thomas Lane, and she was committed for trial at the Guildford Assizes. Here she was acquitted, on the evidence of a minster who knew her well.

There seems to be no real reason for supposing that she had ever practised witchcraft against Hathaway or any one else, but the verdict was extremely unpopular. It was openly asserted that grave injustice had been done, and that both judge and jury had been bribed. Bands of angry men and women besieged Sarah Murdock's house, threatening to duck her in the river, or otherwise force her to remove the spell. Hathaway's fits became much worse. He could not eat or drink for forty days (or so he said) and, during part of that time, he was both blind and dumb. He vomited pins very freely in the presence of witnesses, but this, in the end, was his undoing. Pins showered from his mouth and lay about the floor, but one or two people noticed that some of these were quite dry, which seemed strange in the circumstances. He was seen to make a suspicious movement with his hand towards his pocket, whereupon a man who was present seized a jar and held it to his mouth, challenging him to vomit pins into it. Hathaway did his best, but no pins came, though plenty were found upon him immediately afterwards when, at the demand of the suspicious minority, he was searched.

He was arrested, and brought to trial before Chief Justice Holt. In spite of the exposure concerning the pins, most of his neighbours came to give evidence for him, swearing that they themselves had seen him smitten with blindness, or unable to eat, and that only after he had scratched Sarah Murdock's face did he gain any relief from his sufferings. Some also swore that he had actually vomited pins in their presence without shadow of imposture. But the detailed and exhaustive cross-examination of the Lord Chief Justice was too much for most of them, and many were obliged to withdraw, or contradict, their own evidence. Hathaway was condemned for perjury and fraud, and so his career as a bewitched and suffering individual was ended by a fine, a year's imprisonment, and three appearances in the pillory.

The popular rage against witches continued to burn fiercely among the generality of the people long after the more thoughtful men of the age had begun to doubt the possibility of their alleged crimes. The belief in witchcraft died very hard, but Addison probably expressed the views of many enlightend people at the end of the seventeenth century and the beginning of the eighteenth when he wrote, 'I believe in general that there is, and has been, such a thing as Witch-craft; but at the same time, can give no Credit to any particular Instance of it'.[5]

Most ordinary people could, however, give the most generous credit to any instance with which they happened to come in contact, and nearly every well-known witch-trial was an occasion of great popular excitement. In 1682, three poor women of Bideford – Susannah Edwards, Temperance Lloyd and Mary

Trembles – were brought to Exeter, to be tried for alleged witchcraft. In his account of this trial, Roger North says,

> . . . The women were very old, decrepit, and impotent, and were brought to the assizes with as much noise and fury of the rabble against them as could be shewed on any occasion. The stories of their acts were in everyone's mouth, and they were not content to belie them in the country, but even in the city where they were to be tried miracles were fathered upon them, as that the judges' coach was fixed upon the castle bridge, and the like. All which the country believed, and accordingly persecuted the wretched old creatures. A less zeal in a city or kingdom hath been the overture of defection and revolution, and if these women had been acquitted, it was thought the country people would have committed some disorder. The trial was before Judge Raymond,* a mild passive man, who had neither dexterity nor spirit to oppose a popular rage, and so they were convict and died.[6]

All three prisoners confessed to witchcraft of various kinds, and all three were hanged on 25 August 1682. Two years later, in 1684, Alice Molland perished in the same city for the same offence. This is usually supposed to be the last execution for witchcraft to take place in England, though it was not by any means the last death to be caused by it there.

In 1712, a fierce warfare of pamplets broke out over the case of Jane Wenham, of Walkern, in Hertfordshire. She was a wisewoman in that village, and when a local farmer called her a witch, she complained to Sir Henry Chauncy, a nearby magistrate. He referred the quarrel to the clergyman of the parish, who ordered the farmer to pay the wisewoman one shilling in compensation for the insult. She was not satisfied with this settlement, and doubtless said so, perhaps rather too freely, but there was nothing she could do about it. However, a short time afterwards, Ann Thorn, one of the parson's servants, began to complain of cats scratching and mewing at her door, and of companies of these animals appearing at her bedside. She was also (or so she said) troubled by visions of Jane Wenham,

*Sir Thomas Raymond, of Bowers-Giffard, Essex.

sometimes in her own shape, and sometimes in the form of a talking cat, which bore a knife and urged the girl to kill herself with it. This wild story was corroborated in part by James Burville, who said he had seen the cats outside the door, and that one of them had a face like Jane Wenham.

Other accusations were made against her, including one of magically forcing Ann Thorn to run half a mile at the rate of eight miles an hour, when she was lame after an accident. Strong local feeling was roused against the wisewoman, and so many people came forward to accuse her of various misdoings, that the authorities were obliged to take notice of the matter. She was arrested and brought to trial before Sir John Powell. He clearly was not impressed by the evidence put before him, and did his best to make the jury acquit her. In this he failed, and his well-meant efforts only intensified the local fury against her. The jury convicted her and, as the Law then stood, he had no option but to sentence her to death. He was, however, able to delay the execution, and during the respite so gained, he managed to obtain a royal pardon for her. Her enraged accusers declared that the unfortunate Ann Thorn was still bewitched; and the general interest in the case was so widespread that a fierce battle of leaflets and letters broke out, and continued to rage for some time after the legal proceedings were ended. Jane Wenham lived on for another twenty years, though not in her own parish, where she was always thereafter considered a witch, notwithstanding the royal pardon. She was supported by a small pension from some charitable and, presumably, sceptical individuals in the district. She is said to have lived in a cottage found for her at Hartingfordbury by the Squire of Gilston, and also to have received help, later on, from Earl Cowper of Panshanger.

As late as 1717, no less than twenty-five excited persons came forward to testify at Leicester Assizes against Jane Clarke, her son, and her daughter, all of Great Wigston. They were forced to submit to certain tests, including swimming, and having blood 'drawn above the breath', and most people in Great Wigston were certain of their guilt; but there was no trial, for the Grand Jury at Leicester refused to return a true bill. By then, the persecution mania was already drawing to its close in legal circles, and, only nineteen years later, witchcraft had ceased to be a statutory crime. By an Act of Parliament passed in the ninth year of George II's reign (1736), King James' Act of 1604 was repealed, and it was laid down that, from and after 24 June 1736, 'no Prosecution, Suit, or Proceedings, shall be commenced or carried on against any Person or Persons for Witchcraft, Sorcery, Inchantment, or Conjuration, or for charging another with any such Offence in any Court whatsoever in Great Britain'.

Thus, it was no longer possible to prosecute anyone for bewitching any person, or his goods, or for any other form of alleged witchcraft, and still less, of course, was it possible for any one to suffer death or imprisonment for such a crime. The Act did provide for the prosecution of those who pretended to possess or use magical powers, but it was, of course, the pretence which constituted the offence, and not the actual witchcraft. It is true that the Act was not popular at the time, for much water had yet to flow under the bridges before the people as a whole ceased to believe in, and fear, witches. Many at the time thought it a dangerous and irreligious law, which flouted the teaching of the Bible, including even so great and good a man as John Wesley. But the new law and the ideas from which it sprang had come to stay, and although it could not entirely eliminate violence, it could, at least, by removing the excitement of public trials and the possibility of legal vengeance upon enemies, do a great deal to hasten its decline.

*'At first Ruth Osborne floated, but a man named Thomas Colley . . .
waded into the water and thrust her down with a stout stick'*

12 The Ebbing Tide

The Act of 1736 swept away the penal laws against witchcraft,
but it could not so easily sweep away the beliefs of centuries, nor
could it persuade any one who did not think so already that his
or her ills were due to natural causes, and not to sorcery. If most
educated people had, by 1736, ceased to take witchcraft very
seriously, this was not yet true of the illiterate masses. For the
most part, these were still afraid of the power of witches, and
since they were now unable to seek legal protection against it,
they tended all the more readily to take the law into their own
hands. The passage of many years and innumerable prosecutions
for assault were needed before the ordinary man could be
persuaded that to throw a suspected witch into a pond to see if
he or she would sink or swim, or to scratch his face or arms in
order to draw blood, was anything more than a quite reasonable
and altogether justifiable remedy against evil magic. As late as

1885, the Revd. R. M. Heanley was asked by a wheelwright at Wainfleet Bank to 'say a few words' over the latter's sow, which had been overlooked, and was ailing. The man explained that he could cure the beast himself quite simply by drawing the witch's blood, but he dared not do so because the Spilsby magistrates were 'so ignorant' that they would fine him if he did.[1]

In 1751, an outburst of mob violence in Hertfordshire resulted in the deaths of an old couple named John and Ruth Osborne. A publican named Butterfield, who lived at Tring, had an idea that these two (but especially the woman) had bewitched him, so that not only did his calves fall ill, but he himself began once again to suffer from the fits which had afflicted him in his youth. He declared that during the 1745 rebellion, while Prince Charles Edward was actually marching southwards, Mrs Osborne had come to his door, begging for buttermilk. He refused to give her any, saying he had not enough for his own hogs, whereupon she retorted that the Pretender would get him, and his hogs as well. This was probably no more than an ill-natured wish, but Butterfield seems to have regarded it as a potent curse. When a little later, first his calves, and then he himself fell ill, he had no doubt at all that these misfortunes were directly due to the witch's malice.

He told his friends about it, and most of them agreed that the Osbornes were indeed witches, and that he was their innocent victim. In the course of many agitated discussions at the Inn, it was decided that the guilty pair must be swum. Butterfield had some confused idea that it would be quite legal to do this, provided it was done openly, so he and his friends arranged for the event to be proclaimed by the Town Criers of Leighton Buzzard, Winslow, and Hemel Hempstead. It is a curious fact that no magistrate, or other responsible person, in these towns took any notice of the proclamation, or tried to stop the swimming. No doubt Butterfield and his cronies seriously believed in the efficacy of swimming as a proof of guilt or innocence in matters of witchcraft; but when the day came, matters got badly out of hand, and what was intended as an appeal to the judgement of Heaven turned into the cruel murder of an old woman by an enraged and violent mob.

By this time, the two Osbornes, both of whom were over seventy years old, were lodged in the workhouse. When the parish officials heard what was planned, they hastily moved the old couple into the church, for safety, but this move was not enough for their protection. When a large and excitable crowd arrived at the workhouse and found their victims were not there,

Uncertainty

they burst into the building and tore through every room in the house, doing a great deal of damage as they went. A writer in the *Gentleman's Magazine* (1751) relates that they 'broke the

Workhouse windows, pulled down the pales, and demolished part of the house; and seizing the governor threatened to drown him and fire the town, having straw in their hands for the purpose.'

So great a manifestation of violence was too much for the courage of the local officials. 'For public safety', as it was afterwards explained, the wretched couple were handed over to the screaming mob. They were dragged for two miles to the water at Long Marston, and were there stripped of their clothes and flung into the pond, with their thumbs and great toes tied together crosswise in the traditional manner. At first, Mrs Osborne floated, but a man named Thomas Colley, a chimney-sweep, waded into the water and thrust her down with a stout stick. After she had been thus pushed down three times, she was thrown out on to the bank, with her nose and mouth choked up with mud, and died almost at once, a fact which did not prevent the more savage men in the crowd from beating and kicking her as she lay dead on the bank. Her husband was not quite so far gone when he was taken out of the water, but he died later from his injuries.

Although the Coroner's inquest which followed found some thirty people guilty of wilful murder, only one man was subsequently hanged for it. This was Thomas Colley, against whom it was said in evidence that, after the death of Ruth Osborne, he 'went among the spectators and collected money for the pains he had taken in showing them sport'. He was executed in the following August, his body being subsequently hung in chains as a token, as the Judge observed at the trial, that the life of a witch was no less sacred than that of any other person. This warning seems to have been necessary. In the account of the affair given by the *Gentleman's Magazine* (1751), it is recorded that

> the infatuation of the greatest part of the country people was so great that they would not be spectators of his death (perhaps from a consciousness of being present at the murder as well as he); yet many thousands stood at a distance to see him go, grumbling and muttering that it was a hard case to hang a man for destroying an old wicked woman that had done so much mischief by her witchcraft. . . .

Faith in swimming as a form of water-ordeal for witchcraft

lasted a long time. The *Daily News* for 22 June 1880 reported that Charles and Peter Brewster, who were father and son, were charged at Dunmow Petty Sessions with molesting Sarah Sharpe, of High Easter, 'in a manner likely to lead to a breach of the peace'. Their defence was that the woman was a witch, and that she had bewitched the son's house so that his animals died, his furniture was disturbed, his bed rocked like a boat at sea, and strange shadows were seen in the bedroom. Applications for help made by the father to various wisewomen and cunning men in the district had no useful results, and finally the two men attempted to swim the witch themselves. They were bound over to keep the peace for six months, and probably this was the end of the matter, for no further trouble between the Brewsters and the witch seem to be recorded.

Sometimes a person accused, or suspected, of witchcraft would ask to undergo the swimming ordeal, in order to prove his innocence. In 1785, the *Gentleman's Magazine* reported that

about the latter end of last month, a poor woman of Mear's Ashby, Northamptonshire, being suspected of witchcraft, voluntarily offered herself for trial. The vulgar notion is, that a witch, if thrown into the water, will *swim;* but this poor woman, being thrown into a pond, sank instantly and was with difficulty saved. On which the cry was, *No witch! No witch!*

Isaac Stebbings, of Wickham-Skeith, in Suffolk, was not so fortunate in 1825. He was a huckster, who was suspected, though for no very clear reason, of bewitching two of his neighbours who happened to be mentally afflicted. One of these, a woman, stated that while a traditional witch-detecting charm was being performed at her house, to find out who it was that had overlooked her, Stebbings suddenly came to her door. This, in her view and that of those with her at the time, was clear proof that he was the witch responsible for her mental confusion. His reply to this was that he had gone there selling mackerel, though, rather curiously, at four o'clock in the morning, before the family were up and about. Other local misfortunes began to be ascribed to him also, and at last, losing patience, he proposed that the question of his guilt or innocence should be settled, once and for all, by his voluntarily undergoing the swimming test.

Accordingly, one Saturday afternoon, he was twice ducked in Grimmer Pond in the presence of an interested gathering of local people. Unfortunately, he did not sink, although at the second attempt, four men pressed upon his chest. His head went down then, but his heels came up, and when the pressure was relaxed, he simply floated on his back, as before. After enduring these well-meaning efforts to help him sink for forty-five minutes, he was taken out of the water in a state of exhaustion. However, the spectators were not satisfied, and Stebbings himself must have been bitterly disappointed, since he was determined to establish his innocence of sorcery, and this the test had not done. Another swimming was therefore arranged for the following Saturday, and news of it spread like wildfire through the neighbourhood. It never took place, however, for the rector and churchwardens of the parish stepped in and forbade it before the appointed day came round.[2]

A case of swimming with a tragic end took place in 1863 at Sible Hedingham, in Essex. A queer old man lived there, a foreigner, usually supposed to be French, who was known as Dummy because he could not speak, his tongue having been cut out many years before, though when, or in what circumstances no one knew. He lived alone in a poor hut, with two or three dogs for company; when he went out, he normally wore three hats at a time, and often two or three coats as well. He had a great reputation as a fortune-teller, presumably answering the questions put to him in writing, or by signs. By 1863, he had lived in Sible Hedingham for about eight years, and during that time he had always been regarded as a more or less harmless individual, who also happened to be a practitioner of some forms of white magic.

One night, when Dummy was in the Swan Inn at Sible Hedingham, a woman named Emma Smith, the wife of a beershop-keeper in the nearby village of Ridgewell, suddenly accused him of overlooking her and causing her to be ailing and unwell for the past nine or ten months. She said he had cast a spell over her because, once, she had refused him a night's lodging in her house, and demanded that he should remove it, repeatedly asking him to come home with her, which she seemed to think necessary for this purpose. When he refused to come and, by signs, denied that he had bewitched her, she became very excited and struck the poor old man, again and again with a stick, pulling his coat, and shrieking out her alleged grievances so that everyone present could hear. There were then some forty or fifty people in the bar, and some seem to have become almost as excited as she. A man named Gibson seized hold of Dummy and began dancing him up and down. Others struck and jostled him, and finally the whole company, led by a young man named Samuel Stammers, and including Emma Smith and her husband, poured out of the inn, and ran down towards the brook in Watermill Lane. Dummy was dragged along with them, and was thrown into the water; when he tried to struggle out on the far side, Mrs. Smith and Stammers ran over a small bridge to meet him, and threw him in again. Once more he crawled out, and once more Stammers seized him and, with the aid of Emma Smith's husband, flung him into the deepest part of the stream. By then, most of those concerned in the affair had begun to calm down, and even Stammers thought at last that he had gone far enough, or perhaps was persuaded to think so by some of the more cautious amongst those present. At all events, he lifted Dummy out of the water and laid him on the bank, where he lay for a while, terrified, exhausted, soaking wet, and covered with mud and slime. When he had recovered a little, he was helped home by two women, and his tormentors dispersed, unaware that the whole ugly and riotous business had been watched by a ten-year-old child named Henrietta Garrod, who was later to bear witness against them at Castle Hedingham Petty Sessions.

Dummy died a month later in Halstead Workhouse, from the combined effects of shock and inflammation of the lungs. He was about eighty years old at the time of the swimming, and the blows and the duckings he received then were too much for him. Mrs Smith and Stammers were charged with unlawful assault at the Petty Sessions, and sent from there for trial at Chelmsford Spring Assizes, where both were sentenced to six months' hard labour. *The Times,* reporting the proceedings at the Petty Sessions, drew attention to the fact that Emma Smith's husband ran his own beer-shop, and that Stammers was 'a master carpenter in a small way of business', and went on to remark, coldly, that

It is a somewhat singular fact that nearly all the 60 or 70 persons concerned in the outrage which resulted in the death of the deceased were of the small tradesmen class, and that none of the agricultural labourers were mixed up in the affair. . . . The whole disgraceful transaction arose out of a deep belief in witchcraft which possesses to a lamentable extent the tradespeople and lower orders of the district.[3]

Another noticeable detail was that while confused memories of 'swimming a witch' were probably present in most people's minds at the beginning of the attack on Dummy, it is obvious that practically every one had forgotten what swimming really meant. No one watched to see whether the unfortunate man floated or sank, or drew any conclusions from what actually happened. A simple lust for violence possessed them all (and, in the case of Emma Smith, a desire for revenge), coloured, no doubt, by a vague, inherited notion that witches dreaded running water.

The ebbing tide of the English witchcraft-belief was marked by a wrack of quarrels, accusations, assaults, and prosecutions. In 1808, Anne Izzard, a reputed witch of Great Paxton in Huntingdonshire, was attacked by a noisy crowd who broke into her house one night, scratched her face and drew blood, and threatened to swim her next day. They alleged that she had overlooked two village girls who had been ailing for about three months. In fact, their ill-health dated from a day in the previous February when they had tried to cross the frozen River Ouse on foot, and one of them had fallen through the thin ice into the bitterly cold water. Anne Izzard was not put to the swimming-test on this occasion, but she was assaulted again within a few days. This time, some arrests followed, and the ringleaders were sent to prison, rather to their own surprise. Later in the year, two women set upon her and scratched her face with a pin, and for this, they too were sent to prison. In the end, the hostility of the village became too great, and Mrs Izzard was forced to leave it. She ended her days at St Neots.[4]

In 1823, Anne Burges, of Wiveliscombe in Somerset, was attacked by Elisabeth Bryant and her two daughters, Elisabeth and Jane, and horribly scratched on the arm with an iron nail. This happened in the presence of a number of villagers who made no effort to help the unfortunate woman, but simply stood and watched the proceedings for about ten minutes, until Anne Burges was finally dragged away by a woman who had been with her when the three Bryants set upon her. At the subsequent trial in Taunton it was stated that Mrs Bryant believed that Mrs Burges had bewitched her daughter. Because of this, she had gone into Devonshire to consult old Baker, a noted wise man who practised there, and find out what she could do to protect her child. He told her to draw the witch's blood, and said this would break the spell. Accordingly, she had done so, and her two daughters had helped her; they were now charged with her with malicious assault. All three were sentenced to four months' imprisonment.[5]

The death of Nanny Morgan in 1857 was almost certainly due to an attempt at 'scoring above the breath' that went wrong. This was the defence put forward by the young man who killed her, and it seems very likely it was true. Nanny Morgan lived at Westwood Common, near Wenlock in Shropshire, and was generally believed to be a witch. As a girl, she had been imprisoned for stealing, and when she was released, she joined a band of gypsies for a time. From them she learnt how to tell fortunes, and use certain charms and incantations. When, eventually, she returned to her father's house at Westwood Common, she already had a reputation as a witch, and was supposed to have the Evil Eye. The local people were all afraid of her and took great care not to offend her, and outsiders came to consult her from near and far. After her death, many letters relating to her practice as a magician were found in her house, together with pieces of jewellery which were probably given to her in payment. She is said to have kept a box of toads under her bed, and these, of course, were popularly regarded as her familiars.

She had a lodger, a young man named William Davies, who had stayed in her house for a long time, and now wished to leave it. He did not, however, because he was afraid that she would overlook him if he did. His situation was widely discussed in the village, and one or two people advised the young man to free himself by the time-honoured remedy of drawing the witch's blood. One September day in 1857, when Nanny Morgan was sixty-eight years old, William Davies was seen issuing from the

house with, as it was afterwards alleged, bloodstains on his
clothes. He was not seen again that day, and when one or two
of the bolder villagers summoned up the courage to enter Nanny
Morgan's cottage, they found her lying dead on the floor. Her
face, neck, and arms were disfigured with knife-wounds. Davies
was arrested and charged with murder. He admitted that he had
killed her, but declared that he had never intended to do so, only
to draw blood in the old manner because she was a witch, and
had bewitched him. But she was a strong and active woman, and
he was armed with a knife, and in the struggle that followed his
first assault, he had accidentally killed her. It is a curious sign of
the fear and dislike which Nanny Morgan inspired in her own
village that, after her death, no one could be found to lay her
out, and she had to be buried in the clothes and the shoes she
was wearing when she died.

In 1879, William Bulwer, of Etling Green in Norfolk, was
charged at East Dereham Petty Sessions with assaulting and
abusing an eighteen-year-old girl named Christiana Martins,
who lived in the same parish. This girl stated in evidence that he
had come to her and started to abuse her without any
provocation; she retorted in kind, and the quarrel passed from
words to blows. Bulwer struck her on the hand with a stick.
When asked by the magistrate what she thought was the cause
of this sudden assault and abuse, she said she knew of no reason
whatsoever for it, and to this statement she adhered throughout
the proceedings.

William Bulwer had a different tale to tell. He declared that
the girl's mother was a malevolent witch, and she was just as
bad. He said, very angrily:

Mrs Martins is an old witch, gentlemen, that's what she is,
and she charmed me, and I got no sleep for her for three
nights, and one night at half-past eleven o'clock, I got up
because I could not sleep, and went out and found a
walking-toad under a clod that had been dug with a three-
pronged fork. This is why I could not rest; she is a bad old
woman, and her daughter is just as bad, gentlemen. She would
bewitch any one; she charmed me and I got no rest day and
night for her, till I found this walking-toad under the
turf. . . .[6]

The Chairman of the Bench asked the local police superintendent whether Bulwer was quite sane, and was told that he was; and of course, there is no reason for supposing otherwise. He was simply giving expression to old traditional beliefs that were once practically universal in that district, and may still have been shared, if only in secret, by many of his neighbours. Sixty-eight years later, in 1947, a rather similar case was heard in the same court. Gordon Sutton, an Army pensioner living at East Dereham was summoned for assaulting Mrs Spinks, who was his neighbour. He did not deny the charge, but justified his action by asserting that she had bewitched him. 'A witch has been in the witness-box', he told the magistrates after she had given her evidence, and went on to say, 'Many a time she has tied a bunch of flowers on my front gate, and I have spat on them and thrown them away.'* And he added darkly, 'I dare not tell you half the terrible things she has done to me. I have been tortured for five years.' Mrs Spinks, who was an old age pensioner, denied that she had ever practised any witchcraft upon Sutton, or any one else, but admitted that they had quarrelled over some parsley. The magistrates bound them both over to keep the peace for six months.[7]

There are other stories that show how slowly the old beliefs faded from men's minds, especially in rural areas. At Fressingfield, in 1890, a baby died suddenly, and at the subsequent inquest, it was stated that the death was due to shock, caused by the external use of some powerful irritant. What this was, and why, or by whom it had been applied does not seem to have been made clear. The child's parents, however, had other views. Both swore that the little girl had been overlooked by her step-grandmother, Mrs Corbyn, who had died on the same day. As she lay dying, she told them that the child would not long survive her; nor did she, for a few hours later, she suddenly died. The baby's grandfather, George Corbyn, said in evidence that he had always believed his late wife to be a witch, and for that reason he had always done his best to avoid offending her.[8]

At about the turn of the century, a woman named Anne Blackmore lived by the bridge over the Danesbrook at

* From time immemorial, human spittle has been regarded as a strong defence against evil.

Withypool in Somerset. She was said to be a witch, and to have, amongst other gifts, the power of charming horses. If any one who passed her house happened to annoy her, she would retaliate by bewitching his horses immediately, making them sweat and plunge and become completely unmanageable until she chose to release them. She had other powers as well, and most people were afraid of her.

On one occasion, a farmer's wife had the idea that Anne Blackmore had overlooked her. She therefore turned for help to the local doctor, a man universally trusted and admired in the district, who came of a family that had lived there for several centuries. It was widely believed that he had healing powers of his own, over and above his skill as a qualified doctor. He himself made no such claim, but practically every one believed it to be true. In this case, the farmer's wife asked him to call and see her every Monday morning, and this he did for a long time. He did not treat her medically in any way, but simply looked in with some cheery greeting and then went away again; but as long as he continued to do this, she believed herself to be safe from Anne Blackmore's power. Then, one Monday morning, she told him he need not trouble to come any more. The witch had died and her spell with her, and she was no longer in danger.[9]

Anne Blackmore was not the only witch who was known for her power over horses. In her *Shropshire Folklore* (1883), Charlotte Burne tells the story of Priss Morris, who lived at Cleobury North in the middle of last century. She could stop horses at will and keep them stationary for as long as she liked, though the driver or rider thrashed them and shouted at them, or did his best to cajole them. A farmer whose horses she had thus bewitched threatened to thrash her with his heavy waggoner's whip unless she immediately lifted the spell. He demanded that she should do so by saying 'God bless you and your horses', but this she would not do. All she would say was 'my god bless you and your horses', a form of words which had no effect whatever upon the enchanted animals. Their enraged owner swore he would have nothing to do with her god; he was a worshipper of the true God, and to Him alone must the witch appeal. At last, after many more threats and much abuse, she gave way, and repeated her blessing, leaving out the word 'my'.

The horses were at once freed, and moved forward without further difficulty. Witches were not infrequently required to release a bespelled person or animal by pronouncing a blessing upon them; but in this story there seems to be an additional harking-back to the earlier tradition of the witch as a worshipper of the Devil, or of some alien god.

Gradually and slowly, the old, deep-seated dread of the black witch died away, and with it, the almost universal fear of offending him, or her. As late as 1906, Mrs Leather was told by a man living at Weobley that he had once rashly gone to the help of a policeman who was trying to take the drunken son of a local witch to gaol, and had afterwards regretted it. 'I helped him', he said, 'and didn't think. My missis said when I come home I'd be sorry for it. Sure enough, my pig died next week.'[10] This could hardly happen today, even in remote and unsophisticated districts, for faith in malevolent witchcraft is comparatively rare nowadays, and even where it exists, does not seem to call forth such strong fears as it once did. Wisewomen and cunning-men are not yet altogether unknown, though some of their ancient functions have disappeared now. Wart-charmers and magical healers still flourish in many parts of the country, and so do blood-charmers. Of late years also, there have been, and are, a number of people who openly assert that they belong to a witch-cult, of which the rituals, beliefs, covens, and magical knowledge are directly derived from the witch-rites and beliefs of long ago. If this claim to antiquity of origin is not easily proven, there is no doubt that these modern magicians believe in their powers as firmly as did any of their predecessors, though they do so with less dangers, since to be a witch is no longer against the Law.

The latest, and most probably the last, English Act of Parliament relating to witchcraft is the Fraudulent Mediums Act, which was passed in 1951. The Georgian Act of 1736, which it replaces, removed witchcraft as such from the Statute Book, and made it impossible for any one to be prosecuted for 'Witchcraft, Sorcery, Inchantment or Conjuration', but nevertheless allowed prosecution, with quite severe punishment, for those who pretended to practise these arts, 'whereby ignorant persons are frequently deluded and defrauded'. By it, cunning-men, wisewomen, healers, mediums, crystal-gazers, spiritualists, and fortune-tellers were all put at risk, however innocent and helpful their intentions. By the new Act, their activities are only punishable if they are definitely fraudulent, and done 'for reward'.

And so vanishes the last legal trace of that witch-persecution which was only beginning to decline 300 years ago, and was in its full vigour in the great days of Elizabeth I. If it would, perhaps, be too rash, even yet, to assert that no one in this country ever practises magic now for good or for evil, or secretly consults a white witch in times of difficulty, it can be safely assumed that the majority of Englishmen no longer believe in witchcraft, and are not consciously afraid of it. Traces of the old faith continue to flourish in our everyday superstitions; but the fear and hatred that once gave popular support to the persecution of witches has gone now, and they are not likely to return.

Select Bibliography

Addy, S. O. *Household Tales, with Other Traditional Remains collected in the Counties of York, Lincoln, Derby and Nottingham,* 1895

Ady, Thomas *A Candle in the Dark,* 1655

Atkinson, J. C. *Forty Years in a Moorland Parish,* 1892

Aubrey, J. *Remaines of Gentilisme and Judaisme,* 1686-7 ed. J. Britten, 1881
Miscellanies Upon Various Subjects, 1696 (5th ed. 1890)
Brief Lives, ed. J. Clark, 1898

Baines, E. *History of the County Palatine and Duchy of Lancaster,* 1838

Baxter, Richard *Certainty of the World of Spirits,* 1691

Billson, C. J. *Leicestershire and Rutland,* County Folk-Lore Vol. 1, 1895

Blount, Thomas, *Law Dictionary,* 1717, Antiquarian Repertory

Bray, Mrs A. E. *The Borders of the Tamar and the Tavy,* 1879, 2nd ed.

Briggs, K. M. *Pale Hecate's Team,* 1962

Burne, C. S., and Jackson, G. *Shropshire Folk Lore,* 1883

Burton, Robert *The Anatomy of Melancholy,* 1621

Casaubon, Meric *A True and Faithful Relation of what Passed for many Years Between Dr. John Dee . . . and Some Spirits,* 1659

Collection of Rare and Curious Tracts relating to Witchcraft, 1838

Dalton, Michael *The Country Justice,* 1630 (3rd ed.)

Darrell, John *A True Narrative of the Strange and Grevous vexation by the Devil of 7 Persons in Lancashire,* 1600

Davies, R. Trevor *Four Centuries of Witch-Beliefs,* 1947

Denham, M. A. *The Denham Tracts,* 2 vols, ed. J. Hardy, 1892, and 1895

Devonshire Association, Transactions of

Ewen, C. L'Estrange *Witch-Hunting and Witch Trials,* 1929
Witchcraft and Demonianism, 1933
'A Noted case of Witchcraft at North Moreton, Berks, in the early 17th Century', *Berkshire Archeological Journal,* vol. 40, No. 2, 1936

Fairfax, Edward *A Discourse of Witchcraft: As it was enacted in the Family of Mr Edward Fairfax of Fuystone in the County of York in the year 1621,* 1622 (Reprinted Philobiblon Society – Miscellanies, vol. 5, 1858-9)
Folklore: Journal of the Folklore Society
Frazer, J. C. *The Golden Bough,* 1913-15
Fuller, Thomas *The Church History of Britain: from the Birth of Jesus Christ untill the year 1648,* 1655

Gardiner, Ralph *England's Grievance Discovered in Relation to the Coal Trade,* 1655
Gardner, G. B. *Witchcraft Today,* 1954
Gaule, John *Select Cases of Conscience Touching Witches and Witchcraft,* 1646
Gentleman's Magazine
Giffard, George *A Dialogue concerning Witches and Witchcraftes,* 1593
Glanvil, Joseph *Sadducismus Triumphatus. Or a full and plain Evidence concerning Witches and Apparitions,* 1689
Gratton, J. H. S. and Charles Singer *Anglo-Saxon Magic and Medicine,* 1952
Gurdon, Lady C. E. *Suffolk,* County Folk-Lore, vol, 1, 1895

Hale, Sir Matthew *A Collection of modern relations concerning witches and witchcraft,* 1692
Hale, W. H. *A Series of Precedents and Proceedings ... from Act-Books of Ecclesiastical Courts in the Diocese of London,* 1847
Harland J. and Wilkinson T. *Lancashire Folk-Lore,* 1867
Harrison, G. B. (ed.) *The Trial of the Lancaster Witches,* 1929
Harsnet, S. *A Discovery of the Fraudulent Practises of John Darrell ... ,* 1599
Heanley R. M. *The Vikings: Traces of Their Folk-Lore in Marshland,* Saga Book of the Viking Club, 1902

Henderson, W. *Notes on the Folklore of the Northern Counties of England and the Borders,* 1866, 1879

Higden, Ranulf *Polychronicon,* ed. J. R. Lumby

Historia Rerum Anglicarum, English Historical Society, 1856

Hole, Christina *A Mirror of Witchcraft,* 1957

Holinshed, Raphael *Chronicles of England, Scotlands and Irelande,* 1587

Holworthy, R. *Discoveries in the Diocesan Registry, Wells,* n.d.

Hone, William *The Year Book,* 1845

Hopkins, Matthew *The Discovery of Witches,* 1647

Hughes, Pennethorne *Witchcraft,* 1952

Hutchinson, Francis *An Historical Essay concerning Witchcraft,* 1718

James I *Daemonologie,* 1597

Kirk, Robert *The Secret Commonwealth of Elves, Fauns and Fairies,* 1691, ed. Andrew Lang, 1933

Kittredge, G. L. *Witchcraft in Old and New England,* 1929

Lawes against Witches and Coniuration and some brief Notes and Observations for the Discovery of Witches ... Published by Authority, 1645

Lea, H. C. *Materials towards a Study of Witchcraft,* 1939

Leather, E. M. *The Folk-Lore of Herefordshire,* 1912

Moore Rental, The Chetham Society, XII, 1847

More, George *A True Discourse concerning the certaine Possession and Dispossession of 7 persons in one familie in Lancashire*

Murray, M. A. *The Witch-Cult in Western Europe,* 1921
The God of the Witches, 1933

North, Roger *Lives of the Norths,* ed. A. Jessop, 1890

Notestein, W. *A History of Witchcraft in England from 1558-1718,* 1911

Parrinder, G. *Witchcraft,* 1958

Perkins, W. *A Discourse on the Damned Art of Witchcraft,* 1608

Pitcairn, Robert *Criminal Trials in Scotland,* 1833

Potts, Thomas *The Wonderfull Discoverie of Witches in the Countie of Lancaster,* 1613, ed. G. B. Harrison, 1929

Raine, J. (ed). *Depositions from the Castle of York relating to Offences committed in the Northern Counties in the Seventeenth Century*, Surtees Society, 1861

Remy, Nicolas *Demonolatria*, 1595; ed. Revd. Montagu Summers, 1930

Robbins. R. H. *The Encyclopaedia of Witchcraft and Demonology*, 1959

Rose, Elliot *A Razor for a Goat*, 1962

Russell, J. E. *Witchcraft in the Middle Ages*, 1972

Scot, R. *The Discoverie of Witches*, 1584

Scott, Sir Walter *Letters on Demonology and Witchcraft*, 1830

Sinclar, George *Satan's Invisible World Discovered*, 1685

Smith, Charlotte Fell *John Dee (1527-1608)*, 1909

Sprenger, J. and Institoris, H. *Malleus Maleficarum*, 1499; ed. M. Summers, 1948

Stearne, John *Confirmation and Discovery of Witchcraft*, 1648

Storms, G. *Anglo-Saxon Magic*, 1948

Stow, John *Annales, or A General Chronicle of England, Begun by John Stow; Continued and Augmented ... unto the end of this present yeere, 1631. By Edmund Howes, Gent*, 1631

Summers, Montagu *The History of Witchcraft and Demonology*, 1926

Tebbutt, C. F. *Huntingdonshire Folk and Their Folklore*, n.d.

Webster, John *The Displaying of Supposed Witchcraft*, 1677

Williams, Charles *Witchcraft*, 1941

Notes

Chapter 1

1 *Ancient Laws and Institutes,* quoted in C. L'Estrange Ewen, *Witch Hunting and Witch Trials,* 1929.
2 J. Giles, *Scriptores Rerum Gestarum Wilhelmi Conquestoris,* 1845.
3 *The Works of Jewel,* ed. Parker Society, 1845-50.
4 *Newes from Scotland: Declaring the Damnable Life & Death of Dr Fian, a Notable Sorcerer, who was burned at Edinburgh in January last, 1591,* London, 1591.
5 Dr Thomas Fuller, *The Church History of Britain: from the Birth of Jesus Christ until the year 1648.*
6 It is sometimes alleged that two women were hanged at Northampton in 1705, and a woman and a child at Huntingdon in 1716. The sole support for these statements rests upon two doubtful pamphlets, now believed to be fictitious. No other contemporary reference to either case is known.
7 *Lawes against Witches and Conivration, and some brief Notes and Observations for the Discovery of Witches. Being very useful for these Times, wherein the Devil reignes and prevailes over the Soules of poor Creatures, in drawing them to that crying Sin of Witchcraft ... Published by Authority,* 1645.
8 J. Aubrey, *Remaines of Gentilisme and Judaisme,* Appendix II, 1686-87, ed. J. Britten, 1881.
9 *State Papers, Dom.,* 1634-35.

Chapter 2

1 Translation from H. C. Lea, *Materials towards a History of Witchcraft,* 1939.
2 William of Malmesbury, *Gesta Regum Anglorum,* ed. William Stubbs, Rolls Series, I.

3 Nicolas Remy, *Demonolatry*, 1595, ed. Rev. Montague Summers, 1930.

4 George Sinclar, *Satan's Invisible World Discovered*, 1685.

5 E. Baines, *History of the County Palatine and Duchy of Lancaster*, 1836.

6 Thomas Potts, *The Wonderful Discoverie of the Witches in the Countie of Lancaster*, 1613, ed. G. B. Harrison, 1929.

7 One of the women whom Anne Armstrong accused of witchcraft.

8 *Depositions from the Castle of York relating to Offences committed in the Northern Counties in the Seventeenth Century*, ed. J. Raine, Surtees Society, 1861.

9 Joseph Glanvil, *Sadducismus Triumphatus, Or a full and plain Evidence concerning Witches and Apparitions*, 1689.

10 Francis Bacon, *Silva Sylvarum*, 1608.

11 Scot's informant.

12 Reginald Scot, *The Discoverie of Witches*, 1584.

13 The Venerable Bede, *Historica Ecclesiastica*, ed. C. Plummer, 1896.

14 *Spalding Club Miscellany*, 1841.

15 *The most wonderfull and true Storie of Alse Gooderidge*, 1597.

16 *Lanercost, Chronicle of*, ed. J. Stephenson, Bannatyne Club, 1839.

Chapter 3

1 *The Moore Rental*, Chetham Society, XII, 1847.

2 Thomas Blount, *Law Dictionary*, 1717, Antiquarian Repertory.

3 Edward Fairfax, *A Discourse of Witchcraft: As it was enacted in the Family of Mr Edward Fairfax of Fuystone in the County of York in the year 1621*. Reprinted Philobiblon Society, Miscellanies, Vol. V, 1858-9.

4 R. North, *Lives of the Norths*, Vol. I, ed. A. Jessop, 1890.

5 *The examination and confession of certaine wytches at Chensforde in the Countie of Essex . . .*, 1566. Reprinted Philobiblon Society, Miscellanies, Vol. VIII, 1864-5.

6 *Ibid. The examination and confession . . .*, etc.

7 A. Gibbons, *Ely Episcopal Records*, 1891.

8   J. Harland and T. T. Wilkinson, *Lancashire Folklore*, 1867.

9   *A True and Impartial Relation of the Informations against Three Witches* .... *Who were Indicted, Arraigned, and Convicted at the Assizes holden for the Countie of Devon at the Castle of Exon, Aug. 14 1682* ... (1682).

10 Robert Kirk, *The Secret Commonwealth of Elves, Fauns and Fairies*, 1691, ed. Andrew Lang, 1933.

11 R. Holworthy, *Discoveries in the Diocesan Registry*, Wells, n.d.

12 *Examination of John Walsh*, 1566.

13 Robert Pitcairn, *Criminal Trials in Scotland*, 1833. 'Feared' in this case means 'frightened'. It was Isabel Gowdie who was frightened of the bulls, and not the other way about.

14 *Historia Rerum Anglicarum*, Eng. Hist. Soc., 1856.

15 Nicolas Remy, *Demonolatry*, ed. Rev. Montague Summers, 1930.

16 George Giffard, *A Dialogue concerning Witches and Witchcraftes*, 1593, Shakespeare Association, 1931.

17 Joseph Glanvil, *Sadducismus Triumphatus*, 1689 (4th ed., 1726).

Chapter 4

1   R. M. Heanley, *The Vikings: Their Folklore in Marshland*, Saga Book of the Viking Club, Vol. III, 1902.

2   C. L'Estrange Ewen, *Witch Hunting and Witch Trials*, 1929.

3   *Fearfull Newes from Coventry* ... , written by Lawrence Southerne of Coventry, 1642.

4   W. H. Hale, *A Series of Precedents and Proceedings ... from Act-Books of Ecclesiastical Courts in the Diocese of London*, 1847.

5   Ranulf Higden, *Polychronicon*, ed. J. R. Lumby, R.S.

6   W. Henderson, *op. cit.*

7   J. Bulwer, Article in *Norfolk Archaeology*, V, 1859.

8   *County Folk-Lore – Suffolk*, ed. Lady E. C. Gurdon, Folk-Lore Society, 1893.

9   *The most strange and admirable discoverie of the Witches of Warboys* ... , 1593.

10 W. H. Hale, *op. cit.*

11 *The Wonderfull Discoverie of the Witchcrafts of Margaret and Philippa Flower* . . . , 1619.
12 W. H. Hale, *op. cit.*
13 Parliamentary Writs, ed. Francis Palgrave, 1827-34, Vol. II.
14 John Stow, *Annales, or A General Chronicle of England, Begun by John Stow: Continued and Augmented with matters Forraigne and Domestique, Ancient and Moderne* . . . *by Edmund Howes,* 1631.
15 *Hereford Times,* 22nd January, 1960.
16 *Norfolk Annals,* ed. Mackie, 1901.

Chapter 5

1 Reginald Scot, *The Discoverie of Witches,* 1584.
2 Rev. John Gaule, *Select Cases of Conscience Touching Witches and Witchcraft,* 1646.
3 *A most Certain, Strange, and true Discovery of a Witch, Being taken by some of the Parliament Forces, as she was standing on a small planck-board and sayling on it over the River of Newbury* . . . Printed by John Hammond, 1643.
4 *Gentleman's Magazine,* 1759.
5 Michael Dalton, *The Countrey Justice,* 1630 edition.
6 *Hist. MSS. Comm. Reports,* XIII.
7 Francis Hutchinson, *An Historical Essay concerning Witchcraft,* 1718.
8 *John Bufton's Diary,* Proceedings of the Essex Archaeological Society, 1855.
9 *Hardwicke Papers.* Brit. Mus. Add. MS. 35838. f. 414.
10 *Register of the Privy Council of Scotland,* 1632.
11 *Register of the Privy Council of Scotland.*
12 Concerning this trial, Hopkins gleefully notes in his *Discovery of Witches,* that ' . . . in our Hundred in Essex, 29 were condemned at once, 4 brought 25 miles to be hanged, where this Discoverer lives, for sending the Devil like a Bear to kill him in his garden . . . '.
13 Francis Hutchinson, *An Historical Essay concerning Witchcraft,* 1718, quoting from John Rivett's letter to the author.

Notes

Chapter 6

1 Thomas Potts, *The Wonderfull Discoverie of Witches in the Countie of Lancaster*, 1613.
2 John Darrell, *A True Narrative of the Strange and Grevous Vexation by the Devil of 7 Persons in Lancashire*. George More, *A True Discourse concerning the certaine Possession and Dispossession of 7 Persons in one familie in Lancashire*.
3 *Depositions from the Castle of York relating to Offences committed in the Northern Counties in the Seventeenth Century*, ed. J. Raine, Surtees Society, 1861.

Chapter 7

1 *A True and just Recorde of the Information, Examination and Confession of all the Witches taken at St. Oses in the countie of Essex ... Written orderly as the cases were tryed by evidence by W. W.*
2 *A True and just Recorde of ... all the Witches taken at St. Oses ...*
3 *The Wonderfull Discoverie of Witches in the Countie of Lancaster*, by Thomas Potts Esquier, 1613. ed. and reproduced by G. B. Harrison, *The Trial of the Lancaster Witches*, 1929.
4 Dr Margaret Murray, *The Witch-Cult in Western Europe*, 1921.
5 *Depositions from the Castle of York relating to Offences committed in the Northern Counties in the Seventeenth Century*, ed. J. Raine, Surtees Society, 1861, *The Denham Tracts*, ed. Dr James Hardy, 1895.
6 Joseph Glanvil, *Sadducismus Triumphatus*, 1689.
7 Joseph Glanvil, *op. cit.*
8 Joseph Glanvil, *op. cit.*

Chapter 8

1 Parliamentary Writs, ed. Palgrave, I.14, note 1.
2 R. Holinshed, *op. cit.*
3 *Chronicles of London*, ed. C. L. Kingsford, 1905.
4 J. de Waurin, *Chronique*.

5   Rolls of Parliament, Vol. VI (9. Edward IV).
6   R. M. Heanley, *The Vikings: Their Folklore in Marshland,* 1902.
7   *An English Chronicle . . .* , ed. J. S. Davies, 1856 (Camden Society, Vol. 64).
8   Robert Carr, then Viscount Rochester.

Chapter 9

1   W. Henderson, *Notes on the Folk Lore of the Northern Counties of England and the Borders,* 1866.
2   Rev. J. C. Atkinson, *Forty Years in a Moorland Parish,* 1891.
3   Henderson, *op. cit.*
4   For an account of the nature of this charm, see George Ewart Evans, *The Horse in the Furrow,* 1960.

Chapter 10

1   J. Aubrey, *Brief Lives,* ed. J. Clark, 1898.
2   Acts of the Privy Council, New Series IV.
3   State Papers, Spanish, 1568-1579, No. 524.
4   J. Aubrey, *Miscellanies upon Various Subjects,* 1696 (5th ed., London, 1890).
5   J. Aubrey, *Miscellanies upon Various Subjects,* 1696 (5th ed., London, 1890).
6   Meric Casaubon, *A True & Faithful Relation Of what Passed for many Years Between Dr John Dee (A Mathematician of Great Fame in Q. Eliz. and King James their Reignes) and Some Spirits,* 1659.

Chapter 11

1   Friedrich von Spee, *Cautio Criminalis,* 1631.
2   C. L'Estrange Ewen, 'A Noted Case of Witchcraft at North Moreton, Berks, in the early 17th Century', *Berkshire Archaeological Journal,* Vol. 40, No. 2, 1936.
3   Edward Fairfax, *Daemonologia,* ed. Wm. Grainge, 1882. Originally published as *A Discourse of Witchcraft as it was acted in the Family of Mr Edward Fairfax,* 1622.

4 *A Tryal of Witches at the Assizes Held at Bury St. Edmonds for the Cy of Suffolk; on the 10 March 1664 Before Sir Matthew Hale, Kt. Taken by a Person then attending the Court,* 1682.
5 *The Spectator,* 11 July 1711.
6 Roger North, *op. cit.*

Chapter 12

1 R. M. Heanley, *op. cit.*
2 *County Folk-Lore: Suffolk,* Vol. I, 1895, ed. Lady E. C. Gurdon.
3 *The Times,* 24 September 1863.
4 C. F. Tebbutt, *Huntingdonshire Folk and Their Folklore,* n.d.
5 William Hone, *The Year Book,* 1845.
6 *Leigh Chronicle,* April 19th, 1879.
7 *News Chronicle,* 6 January 1947.
8 *Sunday Times,* 13 April 1890.
9 Told to the writer by the doctor's daughter, 1939.
10 E. M. Leather, *The Folk-Lore of Herefordshire,* 1912.

Index

Butterfield (publican) 169
Buying Wind 57, 58
Byg, William 148
Byx, Margaret 57

Canon Episcopi 24, 25, 28, 50
Canons of London, 94
Carr, Robert, Earl of Somerset 123
Casaubon, Meric 150, 156
Cautio Criminalis 155, 156
Certainty of the World of Spirits 130, 131
Chandler, Susan 160, 161
Charles I 87
Charles II 12, 18
Chattox, Anne 44, 101, 105, 126
Chelmsford, Essex 41, 42, 56, 81
Chester, Bishop of 86
Chisholm, Alexander 80
Christian Astrology 152
Clarke, Elisabeth 81
——, Jane 19, 79, 166
Cleworth, Lancs 90-3
Cobham, Eleanor, Duchess of Gloucester 118, 119, 121
Cocwra, Samuel 80
Coggeshall, Essex 78
Colley, Thomas 171
Comon, Widow 78, 79
Confirmation and Discovery of Witchcraft 82
Corbyn, Mrs 178
Corner of Old Cornwall 56
Cosyn, Edward 140
Coventry 57, 66, 67
——, Bishop of 27
Cox, Julian 52, 53
Crew, Sir Randolph 16, 157
Cromwell, Lady 61, 62
——, Sir Henry 61, 62
Cullender, Rose 160, 161
Cunning-men *see* White Witches
Curtis, Mr & Mrs 68

Daemonologie 16, 17, 78
Dalok, Elena 57, 62
Dalton, Michael 74
Dancing 36, 37, 108, 110

Darcy, Brian 97
Darling, Thomas 88, 89, 90, 94
Darrell, John 87, 90, 93, 94
Davies, William 176, 177
Dawson, William 129
Dee, Dr 91, 143, 145 *et seq*
Demdike, Old, *see* Southerns, Elisabeth
Demonolatry 29
Demons 23, 26, 33, 50, 93, 100, 105, 138, 144
De Nugis Curialium 26
De Praestigiis Daemonum 154
Derby, Earl of 67, 68
Device, Alison 100, 101, 103, 104, 105
——, Elisabeth 85, 100, 103, 104, 105
——, James 32, 85, 100, 103, 105
——, Jennett 20, 104
——, John 101
Devil, The 14, 24, 25, 27, 28, 29, 30, 31, 32, 35, 38, 40, 44, 45, 50, 51, 57, 81, 82, 92, 108, 109, 110, 127, 128, 149, 155, 158
Devil-worship 27, 28, 31, 34, 36, 54, 107, 114, 180
Devil's Mark 13, 74, 81, 161
Dialogue Concerning Witches 52
Diana 22, 24, 25
Dicconson, Frances 85, 86, 87
Dier, Mrs 142
Discoverie of Witches, The 141, 155
Discourse on the Damned Art of Witchcraft 127, 128
Discovery of Witches, The 81, 82
Displaying of Supposed Witchcraft, The 18, 48, 87, 88, 156
Drawing Blood, 72, 89, 166, 168, 169, 175, 176, 177
Driver, Ellen 45
'Dummy' 173-5
Duncan, Gelie 13
Duny, Amy 160, 162

East Dereham 177, 178
Edward I 27, 28
—— IV 116, 117

Index